Stand Up

Stand Up

a memoir of disease, family, faith & hope

Ken Cruickshank

Columbus, Ohio

Published by Gatekeeper Press
3971 Hoover Rd. Ste. 77
Columbus, OH 43123-2839

For information on press or events, contact Ken through his website: www.KenCruickshank.com

Manufactured in the United States of America

10 9 8 7 6 5 4 3 2 1

Library of Congress Cataloging-in-Publication Data

Name: Cruickshank, Ken, author

Title: Stand Up: a memoir of disease, family, faith & hope / Ken Cruickshank

Identifiers:

Library of Congress Control Number: 2017960080

ISBN (trade paper): 9781619848412
ISBN (hardback): 9781619848405
ISBN (ebook): 9781619848429

BISAC: BIO026000 BIOGRAPHY & AUTOBIOGRAPHY / Personal Memoirs. | BIO017000 BIOGRAPHY & AUTOBIOGRAPHY / Medical. | REL012040 RELIGION / Christian Life / Inspirational.

Subjects: LCSH: Cruickshank, Ken. | Cruickshank, Ken—Philosophy. | MS—Patients—United States—Biography. | Illness. | Life. | Death. | Cruickshank, Ken—Chronic Illness—Psychological Aspects. | Parents—United States—Biography.

Dedications

To my wife, Karen:

Nothing would get written without your
encouragement and support. You are my confidante
and caregiver, my beautiful and talented artiste. No
one loves anything or anyone more than I love you.
Our journey continues . . .

To my children, Ken, Caitlin, and Bre:

I am blessed to call you mine. Any trials I've had, or
may have, are quickly numbed by the great joy you
bring to my life. We've persevered together. May your
futures be grand and fulfilling.

John, Sarah, and Dad: You are missed
Mom: You are special

To the *malades*:
Peace, comfort, love

To my early readers and supporters,
thank you:

Karen, Ken, Caitlin, Bre, Margaret, Celia, Rich,
Beth F, Bob, Fran, Peg, Jim, Cathy, Kathy, John, Kris,
Barbara, Karen A, Mike, Kirk, Kevin, Will, Ron,
Beth G, Dan, Nance, Lesley, Pete, Paul, Suzy, Dale,
Chris, Dave, Yvonne, and Mark

Contents

Preface

GROWING UP IN Orange County, California, as the sixth of ten children, I engaged in endless mischief: launching water balloons, toilet-papering houses, lighting cherry bombs, and burning muscle car rubber. Eventually I ventured off to college and discovered the woman of my dreams (my wife, Karen), and together we raised three children.

In 1992, at age thirty-two, a doctor diagnosed me with something called primary progressive multiple sclerosis, to which I replied, "What the heck is that?" Twenty-five years later, I feel I'm a bit of an expert on the topic of a life transformed by chronic illness.

Stand Up is not a story of the science and medicine of disease; instead, I hope it's an entertaining and inspiring account of overcoming health-related or other trials in one's life. Mine is a tale of lessons learned and wisdom gained as a man, family, and some fascinating souls share a journey to a destination unknown. You are now a part of the experience.

PART I
My Life, My Perspective

Things that happened. Things I contemplate.

CHAPTER 1

Recognizing the Pain

"If you fell down yesterday, stand up today."
—H. G. Wells

Essay by my son, Ken. Jesuit High School, 2005:

He looks tired. He is strong. Is he a broken man, or is he holding onto something?

He lies on the floor, in his underwear, pinned helplessly against the wall. As always when he falls, he pauses afterward without flinching a muscle or uttering a sound. Like two tides clashing against each other, expressions of embarrassment and frustration cloud his face. He tries to decide what to say. He searches for something that will lighten the moment and allow everyone to calm themselves, as he always does.

"Whoops," or "Well that was fun," he would say to pacify the overly emotional conduct of my sisters and mother. But this time is different. My sisters aren't home. He can't think of anything to say. He just looks at me. He seems to pierce straight through my eyes and out the back of my head. His eyes emit the most helpless, disappointed gaze I have ever seen in him. Disappointed in what? Himself. Glaring in front of his eyes, his past taunts him. His agile, powerful legs now lay withered, uncoordinated, and nearly limp in front of him.

His helpless eyes hollow out my insides. But I know what to do. I push any emotion aside, and try to help him with a straight face. Seemingly simple, this task soon becomes a formidable feat. I feel tears forming in the recesses of my skull. Treating them like an invading force, I fight them off with all my strength.

Does he see my pain? Does he see my struggle for composure? I hope not. If given the choice to show my feelings or lie, I will lie.

My innards are being ground up in a meat grinder, but my face does lie. I manage to manufacture a straight expression out of the factory of my face. I force out the only thing either of us has said, "You all right?" with a masterfully stoic air. A euphemistic chuckle trickles out of his mouth, followed with "Oooh yeah." I start over to him, when usually I would put my hand out to help him up. But I can see that this time is different.

With all the strength and coordination left in his body, he lumbers over to his hands and knees. He doesn't want me to help him this time. He wants to prove to himself and to me that he has not been completely overtaken, that he is not yet a cripple. His arms, which still possess some of his youthful strength, reach for the fireplace mantel like a baseball player reaching over the fence for a ball, knowing that disappointment will ensue if he fails.

He grabs a firm hold on the fireplace. His knuckles white with strain. His muscles bulging with exertion. His face red with determination. As he slowly rises, the most powerful force of tears moves in a tornado just behind my eyes. But I fight them off still.

He does not want help this time. He does not give up. His tortuously slow rise comes to an end when I take his hand just in time to prevent another fall. Though his face changes little, I know what he is thinking. "See, I did it, now help me to bed," he said silently. Our overly cautious steps led to the bed where he crashed like a tree onto his covers. As soon as he is in his bed ready to rest, I know I must leave. Unfortunately, he can see this. With only silent recognition, I walk out of the room.

He has always been an example, a model of perfection. But now that my dad isn't perfect, what kind of an example is he? A worse one? Or a better one?

My father was diagnosed with primary progressive multiple sclerosis (MS) in 1992. This disease has often burdened my family and me, being his oldest and only son. Through all of these difficulties, though, my family and I have triumphed and transcended my father's obstacles.

*   *   *

My wife, Karen, informed me our son, Ken, had written the preceding reflection in the aftermath of one of my "falling episodes" inside our home. She cried over his powerful words and wondered whether I had read the soul-baring account. Years passed before I committed to doing so. I was finally prepared to delve into his innermost thoughts, to contrast them with my own.

Attempting to recite Ken's words aloud, I stopped. My throat tightened, I lowered my head, and tears cascaded down my cheeks. His thoughts weighed only ounces: ink pressed onto a few sheets of paper, stapled in one corner, and creased. But what they represented felt heavy. I stared into the forest halted by unexpected emotions, and then I dissected each sentence he'd written.

I remember the incident Ken had written about as if it had happened yesterday. That look in my son's eyes: helplessness, heartbreak. For years, I wondered if it had been a defining moment in his relationship with me. Were my apprehensions an overreaction? After all, I had fallen many times in front of my wife and children. But this father-son moment was different, more personal. It forever affected a son's perspective of his invincible dad, and it exacerbated anxieties about my future, my family's future. Time has passed; I can now recount Ken's version of events without a rash of unbridled sentiments.

As my disease journey unfolded, I learned that an altered reality needed to be embraced, just as failure must be embraced before one achieves success. Hiding for years from my son's impassioned narrative reflected my fears of accepting what I had deemed a dire truth: Aspects of my identity had been stripped away. I was losing the ability to control my life, and I'm a person who likes to be in control. It was frightening.

For years, I remained mired in this selfish perspective. But progress has been made. Internal walls of resistance have been torn down. I accept my situation, *our* situation, and have crafted a new but still fulfilling life, while acknowledging I can no longer manage much of it on my own terms. My enlightenment came in waves, sometimes punctuated by dramatic experiences, but more often through wisdom gained by trial and error as MS battled for control of my mind and body.

Our children have specific recollections related to my disease that are difficult to consider. Nobody wants to see his or her father helplessly taken down a peg or two. During a high school retreat, our oldest daughter, Caitlin, shared her personal experiences of a dad who had been quite active for most of her life, but who was now barely able to walk and would soon be restricted to a wheelchair. Word of the difficult truths she had shared made their way to Karen and me. Caitlin's reflections of living with an ailing father—personal insecurities she had guarded for years—unleashed an outpouring of repressed emotions and tears.

In grade school, our youngest daughter, Bre, wrote a letter to God asking Him to "please take the MS away," assuming it was something tangible that could be yanked from my body and disposed of. Years later, she grew distressed watching me fall hard to the pavement from my scooter in the Virgin Islands, unprepared for another seemingly innocuous moment that might disproportionately affect all our lives. She walked away rigidly as I lay on the ground, weeping and struggling to cope.

All three of our children were forced to see me broken and motionless on our garage floor after a traumatizing fall that changed my life. And of course, Karen has had to deal with the relentless physical, mental, and emotional dynamics related to our MS story.

Progressive diseases are a shared burden, a collective odyssey, and are often more demanding of the caregivers than of the patient. You learn to manage any obstacles as a team. For too long, I wanted to apologize for having unfairly challenged my family with so many difficult moments, even as they knew there was nothing I could have done (or can do) to eliminate those trials.

I do not allow my illness to dictate who I am, or all the terms of how I cope with my uncertain future. This isn't easy; sometimes I fail. Despite everything that must be overcome, a person with MS (an *MSer*) like myself often comes to a surprising conclusion: He realizes his disease has been cleansing, that misplaced priorities have been reset, and that he has become a better person in important ways.

I have learned to manage problems that once seemed too daunting, and I proselytize the truism "life is short, make the best of it." I share hard-earned wisdom with the healthy, and especially among those struggling with disease or misfortune in their own lives.

My family has learned to thrive, to be happy and fulfilled. We appreciate our good fortune while tolerating the burdens progressive illnesses dictate. Each of us has transformed into a more compassionate, stronger, and better human being.

Perhaps inevitably, we have become warriors.

CHAPTER 2

Transcending Disease

Wisdom is neither scarce nor always obvious.

I AM NOT GOING to lie; it's kicking my butt today. Exhausted, I still haven't gotten dressed after my shower two hours ago. I found it difficult to reach for and grab my Harley-Davidson mug filled with coffee; I spilled some of the extra-dark morning kicker onto the cream-colored carpet after the handle had shifted in my weak hand. The face peering back at me in the mirror looks defeated. I want to throw a bunch of expletives at the disease to let it know how I feel (sometimes I do), and to attempt to threaten it into running away like a spooked intruder. I am face-to-face with my opponent; he is powerful and, this day, more easily recognized. I know his ultimate objective: to destroy me. He thinks he has me on the ropes, and to some extent he does. But I feel my resistance to his wickedness building within me, and I know—he knows—I will soon be back in full control. He will never win the war, only a battle here or there. Even if one day it appears he won the war . . . he did not. *I decide* who wins. It's very important that my family and friends understand this; it is a most prized possession: my perspective. The invariable conflict is my psyche versus the evil onslaught of my body. I will retrench in an hour or two. Tomorrow I will be rocking and rolling. But at this particular moment, today's score is: MS 1 and Ken 0.

What defines us? Does a chronic progressive disease form the person, or can one's outlook and perspective alter the manifestations of their illness?

People look at me today and see an unnaturally positioned man motoring through restaurants, stadiums, airports, or churches on a portable scooter. That snapshot is their definition of who or what I am. Even I am surprised by how slowly I move. I am not very strong, have poor balance, and have lost hand dexterity to the point where I can no longer type.

Every so often, thankfully rarely, I hold a private pity party where only Ken Cruickshank is invited. I contemplate whether my own children remember their dad was once quite physically active. That scooter dude used to love rugby, running, baseball, hoops, backpacking, crabbing, fishing, and weekend-warrior competitions of every sort.

Do my daughters wish their father could still dance with them? I remember the first high school father-daughter event where I couldn't hit the parquet dance floor, risking an uncoordinated fall that would have been followed by a rash of difficult emotions. I would have hidden mine. Does our son wish I could jog and lift weights with him? We used to do those things together. Are those vivid memories for him?

Years ago, as my multiple sclerosis was only beginning to affect me in any visible way, I used to joke with Karen that I had become a mere shadow of the athletic man she'd married. I think I was pretending to humorously contend with my declining skills, coordination, strength—and identity. Karen never found anything funny in the "shadow" quip. Perhaps she understood that, beneath the façade, I was struggling, sometimes greatly so. Looking back, I assume my attempts at any self-deprecating humor were instead thinly veiled moments of . . . of what? Fear? Immaturity? Egotism? The answers to all my questions slowly revealed themselves.

There are millions of people like me all around us, individuals who never want to be defined by their illnesses, visible and invisible, but rather by their zest for life. I have always challenged our children to appreciate that the elderly or disadvantaged people they might observe during a typical week in stores, theaters, the park—anywhere—likely have compelling, perhaps even fascinating, histories. Lives full of adventure, simple goodness, debacle, or achievement. You may be such a person.

As an old, dying man, my father once told me he continued to partially view himself as the rowdy twenty-year-old he once was. I could relate. Many of us never lose the spirit of what defined us during our youth. There's a healthy dose of "glory days" in everyone.

Most of our friends and family members have captivating stories to share, moments reflecting the essence of who they are, or were. Listening to their life experiences, their lessons learned, can expose their truest identity and teach us something valuable about *living*.

Perhaps that decrepit soul hunched over with the hand-carved cane was a world-class athlete. That old woman with Alzheimer's may have been an acclaimed artist. The stranger you passed at the retirement home may have had an uncanny ability to grow the most beautiful roses in Portland. The thirty-five-year-old guy in the wheelchair may be an Alabama (or Auburn!) season ticket holder.

I grew up in a huge, spirited family in Orange County, California, in the 1960s and '70s. I traveled extensively from a young age, even alone, and witnessed or participated in some dangerous or ridiculous happenings. Exploits of my youth provide telling backstories that resonate with some listeners and are considered outrageous by others. My journey has been at times punctuated by dramatic events.

Life has been eventful, and I expect my future with Karen to be filled with precious moments, more escapades, and a mutual passion for living. I am hoping for ten grandchildren from our three children (I don't care how they divvy them up). Am I insecure about aspects of that future? Probably, but onward I will march.

The following chapters are presented in five themed sections; the respective episodes and illuminations presented are strands of silk woven into the tapestry of my life, the lives of my family, and fascinating souls who have (sometimes unexpectedly) shared my odyssey. My actions throughout may surprise, impress, or disappoint you. Ultimately, I hope to illustrate how being stricken by aggressive chronic disease, dealing with life's myriad forced transitions, and maintaining hope for the future are fully compatible.

Anyone battling disease or personal hardship is offered a path to optimism. It may be difficult to find, but it's out there, needing to be discovered. I readily advocate that happiness is a state of mind, a conscious pursuit. A decision one makes. As you lay this book down after reading the final page, I hope a positive spirit envelops you. And I hope you smile.

CHAPTER 3

A Mystery Solved

"Do not be afraid; our fate
Cannot be taken from us; it is a gift."
—Dante Alighieri

KAREN AND I moved to Scottsdale, Arizona, in 1988, with our young son Kenny in tow. I had a strong negative reaction to desert landscapes after my arrival to the state as a college student in 1979; though, like Karen, I eventually grew to appreciate the surroundings.

After real estate prices had gone bonkers in Orange County from 1985 through 1988, Karen and I decided to cash in, move to the desert, and buy a beautiful Mediterranean home. I'd start a new career, and we'd live happily ever after. I was twenty-eight years old, sporting not a strand of gray hair, and thought I had everything figured out.

Twelve months later, I left the company that had moved us to Arizona and began working for another firm while simultaneously launching my own business. My family settled comfortably into the sun-drenched lifestyle, and we hold fond memories of our time in Arizona. Kenny bonded with a grandfather he would one day deliver a eulogy for, my father-in-law, Jack. Caitlin was born at Scottsdale Memorial Hospital on Mother's Day, 1989. Our property was set in an indigenous desert development where we dealt with omnipresent rattlesnakes, scorpions, and tarantulas. We reunited with friends from our days at ASU, and with others who had left Orange County for the similar but much more affordable lifestyle in Arizona.

I decided to train for competitive rugby during this time, after five years away from the sport. I hoped my legs might still be fleet enough to earn the wing position for a club out of Tempe managed by an Irish-American rugger well-known in the Southwest, Salty Thompson, a teammate from my ASU years. I had enjoyed many sports as a young man, but playing rugby was the pinnacle of my athletic experiences. There is something magical about the history, traditions, and camaraderie of rugby.

I trained hard, and though I wasn't yet performing at the level desired, I thought I had made real progress. I suited up for a match at a tournament in Tucson after two months of conditioning and ran or tackled well enough during the first half. Then that ubiquitous Arizona sunshine increased the temperatures considerably as the game wore on, and I began to play worse. Salty was snapping at me to get my "stuff" together, saying I was hurting the team. I was.

In 1989, it made little sense to me that I could play well at the beginning of a match, early in the day when it was cooler, versus later in the game after temperatures had risen twenty or more degrees. I continued to practice hard for weeks but I was digressing. It was an uncomfortable time for me; I felt my teammates may have believed my real problem was that I wasn't committed to training, thus my declining performances.

I started going to doctors but they provided no answers. They would ask me to strip down and be staring at a young man who was six-two, two hundred ten pounds, and who appeared quite healthy. Physicians ran various tests over the next two years in

Arizona, and later in California and Oregon, and all of them concluded the same thing: There's nothing wrong with you.

During those frustrating years before age thirty-two, I occasionally fell while stepping into my car, stumbled while walking several times, and dropped beverages in kitchens or restaurants. I would laugh off the episodes. I began losing reflex contests regularly. I became a crappy basketball, softball, and ping-pong player. I was getting waxed by good buddies in every competition imaginable, but always ended each contest with a smirk while demanding, "Come on, one more game." Even though the regular losing was humbling, I still enjoyed the simple pleasures of shooting hoops or throwing a ball. In less than ten years, I wouldn't be able to do those things, at all.

After deciding to reenter the high-tech mainstream during our second year in Arizona, I interviewed with Compaq Computer and Intel Corporation. The Intel division I targeted was headquartered in Oregon, a state Karen and I had visited once while attending a friend's wedding.

Having accepted the job with Intel, we began our lives in the Pacific Northwest in 1991, with Karen eight months pregnant (Bre would be born in Portland, continuing the trend of each of our three children being delivered in different states). We moved into an apartment for a transitional period that was supposed to last up to three months, but the constant banging and loud music in the unit over our heads pushed us to make a joint executive decision after a single night: *We're outta here!*

We found a wonderful house in a Rose City (Portland's nickname) suburb we were instantly drawn to. It was a spec home that had sat empty for months, the perfect opportunity for this business maverick to practice the art of the deal. We offered, countered, and countered again with the builder. Twenty-five hundred dollars separated us from owning the beautiful residence. I told Karen I wasn't budging another buck, that this guy had better accept our latest offer or he's lost qualified buyers. I knew he'd fold; just give him a week or so. Karen's response was, "Oh great. I'm pregnant, looking for doctors, living in a noisy apartment, found a house we love, and we're going to lose it over $2,500 and your stubbornness."

So . . . we bought the house (*without* the $2,500 price reduction). Oregon has been our home for twenty-five years; it was a great place to raise our children.

*   *   *

As our family was growing and our lives mirrored the sort of suburban contentment you see on television, signs of my disease were growing more visible, but mostly to me alone. Tingling sensations were building within my legs and arms, and my dexterity was worsening. Looking at old photos, my left hand was holding wine glasses and coffee cups at tilted angles. The stumbles and falls were increasing in frequency but remained cloaked in humor.

In 1992, I was a thirty-two-year-old focused on rising through the corporate ranks. I had stopped expecting answers to the mystery of my declining health. Of course, I would have preferred having had the puzzle solved, but I told myself if the doctors were not concerned, then perhaps I shouldn't be. Finally, unexpectedly, the answer came.

During a basketball game at an athletic club in downtown Portland, something very odd was happening. My body started to buzz as if I were gripping a low-voltage live wire. Also, my eyesight turned blurry, which I attributed to the sweat dripping down my hair and face. The sensation of being charged by electricity disappeared that afternoon, but my eyesight remained blurred.

My GP sent me to an ophthalmologist, who said I was suffering from optic neuritis; he suggested we wait two weeks to gauge any improvement in my vision. Next, I visited a neurologist who performed a spinal tap, which she later insisted ruled out MS. That specialist sent me back to my GP, who didn't believe the results; he had a strong hunch I had MS, so he sent me to another doctor. Thirty minutes into my meeting with the fourth neurologist I'd seen over a five-year span, the elder physician sat me down to say he'd made a clinical diagnosis: I had something called primary progressive multiple sclerosis (PPMS).

Throughout the ensuing months, I was telling everyone that I was relieved to have been diagnosed with *something*, even if it was a chronic autoimmune disease with no cure. I'd convey that just having answers, knowing my symptoms were real—that they weren't some sort of hallucination—was liberating. But all those words were a half-truth: I was unsettled.

I began to research the potential implications of MS on my future. Would I be able to support my family? Would I become a burden to those I loved most? Would I be wheelchair bound? Would I die young? I was silently struggling with the dire possibilities uncovered through the information and misinformation I was gathering. At the time, I still looked fit as a fiddle . . . but the enemy was encroaching.

CHAPTER 4

Repressed Truth

Unrestrained despair crushes verisimilitude.

THE GALVINS KNEW how to throw a party.

The food was once again stunning at our neighbors' 2004 St. Patrick's Day bash. It always boggled my mind that the Galvins cooked and prepared everything for the annual celebrations by themselves. Incredible hors d'oeuvres, salads, fresh breads, uniquely prepared vegetables, premium entrées, and an impressive assortment of desserts. My words could never do justice describing how truly delectable they were. And of course, no St. Patrick's Day celebration would be complete without the requisite local brews (a Portland specialty), Harp and Guinness lagers, Irish whiskey, wines, and port.

I was having a wonderful time catching up with friends I hadn't seen in months or years. Getting daring, I took a few steps with my shillelagh away from my reserved seat in the kitchen and toward the Irish folk musicians. I stood in that exact spot for the next hour, sipping premium liquors.

The party wound down and Karen readied to depart. I told her I'd follow shortly; some good friends had offered to assist me home. That would have ordinarily been an easy thing to do; after all, "home" for me was next door. My wife left and I socialized a bit longer, listening to live music and chatting away.

About an hour later, I took Robby the Belgian up on his offer to coordinate getting me back to my residence. He grabbed John the Scotsman and Tom the Executive and we prepared to tackle the steps out the front door. I was accompanied by three strong bodies; what could go wrong?

The amble outside was instantly alarming; I could barely stand upright. The nerve signals through my brain and spinal nerve canal were already short-circuited by MS lesions; the alcohol had exacerbated the problem. When we got to my garage, I demanded my friends let go of me, but they were reticent as I seemed oddly imbalanced. Convincing them I was fine (damn those powers of persuasion), they released their grips for a quick moment, just long enough for me to fall backward toward the cement. They grabbed me before I hit with full force, though my head still whiplashed the ground harder than they or I realized (Karen believes I may have sustained a concussion at that point). I could not walk at all, and they carried me and my cane to the front door, rang the chime, and moved me past a concerned wife into our master bedroom. I was laid on our bed and they departed, thus they missed the ensuing drama.

I looked toward the ceiling. All I really remember screaming was, "Why are you doing this to me? Why, why, why? What the hell did I do? Tell me, tell me, dammit! Why are you destroying my life?" Karen welled up in tears, not knowing what to say or do. She thought I might be somehow blaming her for years of frustration and pent-up emotions now being unveiled. I still regret that.

My message was not meant for my adoring wife; I was crying out to God. My unsettled subconscious had intersected my inebriated conscious and revealed itself through an angry, ugly, and selfish outburst. In a weak moment, I unleashed a torrent of deep-seated emotions related to my known and unknown future. Looking back on the eruption, asking God why I had somehow been chosen to be afflicted with this damn disease, the fairer question would have been, "Why not me?" Why should I have been exempted from holding the proverbial short straw?

After the eruption, calm settled and Karen got me ready for a night's rest. I awoke the following morning to a bloody pillow, the result of a head wound from my fall in the driveway. I was not able to stand for the next two and a half days; it scared the heck out of both of us.

I had not consumed an exorbitant amount of alcohol. What transpired had also happened years earlier, at a business function in Georgia. I was drinking a cocktail while standing among a few executives of a distribution company when I inexplicably collapsed while speaking. They helped me up; I offered a startled apology, and they were gracious enough to continue the conversation as if nothing strange had taken place. They knew I had MS, but it was the first business incident displaying an obvious manifestation of the disease. For me, drinking and multiple sclerosis don't mix; a glass of wine is my limit today. The disproportionate effect on my mobility isn't worth two glasses of even the finest cabernet sauvignon (bummer).

In retrospect, I am glad I went through the St. Patrick's Day ordeal. I hope it wasn't too uncomfortable for those I'd departed with; they were just trying to get me home safely. These men had seen my disease impair me at the office or elsewhere, so they understood I was becoming more prone to the unexpected. I realize the episode was terribly distressing for Karen, but it also gave her an honest glimpse of a hurting man, unedited and profoundly personal. Her husband was struggling with an illness he had little control over.

Later that week, I had to remind myself that for every person in my state of deteriorating health, there was someone else with MS, or some other affliction, who was dealing with much direr circumstances than my own. I told myself to get over it.

I still do. Get over it, buddy.

CHAPTER 5

Last Day Walking

If you knew it was going to happen,
why deny the consequences?

A YEAR AFTER THE St. Patrick's Day party, in 2005, I took time off work for what I assumed would be a routine MRI.

Because I am so claustrophobic, the doctor had prescribed a double dose of Valium to ease my anxieties before I lay down. I was about to be slid into the dreaded imaging tube for my brain scan. When they dropped the cage over my head and pushed me into the belly of the beast, I quickly determined an MRI was not in the cards this day, promptly demanding the technicians "get me outta here!" As my MS had worsened, so had my claustrophobia—disproportionately. (I now have difficulty with any cramped spaces, including elevators. Tight quarters instantly trigger sweating and labored breathing. According to my neurologist, this is common for people with advanced MS. Unlike healthy people, we know we cannot free ourselves from certain physical constraints, which can trigger panic.)

Nurse Debbie wheeled me out of the radiology department

to the curbside patient pickup zone, where I again apologized for not being a model patient; I'm sure the RN thought I was a wimp. The MRI would have measured any changes in the number and size of brain and spinal lesions. Over the previous ten months, I had been clinically trialing the cancer medication Rituxan as a potential treatment for multiple sclerosis. (The study ultimately concluded the drug offered no benefit to MS patients, which surprised Karen and me; we were convinced I had improved while on it. Interestingly, later trials proved there were indeed benefits for many MS patients using Rituxan. It is currently being prescribed as a treatment option for those battling relapsing and progressive forms of the disease.)

I got picked up at the hospital by a buddy around 5:15, and we headed straight to Starbucks, a regular destination for this caffeine addict. After ordering my standard Grande Latte with one Splenda, he drove me back to my home for what had been, for this patient whose life-routine had slowed immensely, a very busy day. I grew relaxed as I distanced myself from the hospital, not recognizing that the Valium was still administering its potent chemicals, numbing my senses and body.

The garage door was open as we pulled into my driveway. My friend backed up and I prepared to exit with my coffee and cane; I'd need to walk thirty feet to reach our back door. He drove away as I thanked him for the lift. It then became obvious my strength and coordination had been greatly affected by the now fully-absorbed Valium.

Struggling to keep my body upright, I began to wobble. I told myself to focus, to head in a straight line, and to take small steps. I couldn't control my limbs and I began to stumble; I was picking up speed instead of slowing down, despite my best efforts to do otherwise. My cane was only momentarily delaying the inevitable (*but cane, dear cane, you've been so good to me!*).

The last image I remember, before waking up in a daze on the cement floor, was of falling face-first toward the unforgiving concrete, not realizing that this would be, for me and my family, a life-changing event.

While I'd been falling for years, the number of incidents per week had risen. Subconsciously, I knew it was just a matter of time before I would collapse and break something on my body; I just hoped it wouldn't be too significant. Three "near misses" over the previous two years had been rather unsettling; I uncomfortably acknowledged I could have been killed falling down that long flight of stairs, off that ledge, or into that pit associated with those episodes.

I remember flying forward as if I were trying to tackle someone, and I knew this opponent (cement) would be unforgiving. Thank God my trusty old BMW 635 had a strong, protruding side-view mirror. As I toppled forward and downward, the mirror casing rolled me onto my right side just prior to impact, likely preventing a terrible head injury.

After I regained consciousness (over two hours later), I could see my coffee spilled out in front of me; my cane was stuck beneath my body. I grew convinced I had slammed my head onto the garage floor, but it was instead the force of the total body collapse that had caused my blackout. Many people with multiple sclerosis have little or no ability to mitigate the effects of a fall, a *timberrr* sensation we dread.

I couldn't understand why I was having such difficulty moving my legs and I called out for help, unable to do so loudly. Because no one showed up, I assumed I was home alone. This would be the first episode in my life where I felt totally helpless. As I was lying on the floor and staring at the garage ceiling, I realized I could barely tilt my head left or right. I attempted to pull myself along the surface, but the pain and my weak limbs prevented me from doing so. I had grown to hate being unable to control the outcomes of situations (I've become more used to it), so I lay frustrated by my predicament.

Eventually, I heard a voice in the kitchen and I called out again. Karen opened the door, looked down, and rushed to my side. She screamed for our son, Ken, who was eighteen at the time and had been upstairs watching a movie with the family, to come and assist her. I asked them to keep our daughters, Caitlin and Bre, sixteen and thirteen, out of sight of their father now sprawled out on the cold, hard surface. I wished the kids hadn't been home that evening; I recalled their painful expressions every time I had fallen the previous few years. As the drama unfolded, my girls wept, seeking answers. Daughters want their fathers to be indestructible. Sons do, too.

Though I couldn't view the way my limbs were positioned, I inanely assumed Karen, Ken, and our gardener would somehow succeed at getting me into our bedroom, where I could lie down to recover. Everything would be fine, I argued, I just needed rest! But Karen insisted she call 911, a decision I was *very* displeased with. Turns out she made the right call (again).

It was about 8:30 as the ambulance and fire truck arrived. When my family had attempted to move me earlier, I winced if they nudged my legs even slightly, so I was curious how the professionals were going to transfer me. One of the paramedics grabbed the loose Levi's cotton near my shins and thighs, while the other lifted my upper body. They did a great job; my legs were barely strained through the process. I got lifted onto the gurney, secured, and glided into the ambulance.

Karen clutched her coat and keys before asking Ken to help the girls deal with raw emotions. Bre refused to come in from outside, so our son attempted to console her as the sun set. Karen's last image was of Ken and Bre sitting on the porch, still absorbing the shock. Karen called her parents in Arizona, and mine in California, while she followed the ambulance to St. Vincent's in Portland.

On the way to the hospital, a paramedic asked if I wanted morphine for the pain I was experiencing. I replied that I didn't need anything and that I must have injured some ligaments or tendons, that's all. I felt pain, but my confusion was stunting much of it. In retrospect, I consider what the paramedic replied to be quite humorous: "Well, in my experience and opinion, when one leg is shorter than the other and rotated at ninety degrees, it typically means the patient has broken a hip."

After completing his assessment of my condition, an emergency room doctor also asked me if I needed some morphine. I remained mired in layers of denial, and told the doctor, the nurse, Karen, our good friend Parmie, and anyone else who would listen that whatever was wrong with me required a simple fix, that I'd be out of the hospital in an hour or two.

After a few x-rays, the heretofore good-natured doctor returned to the room and exclaimed, "You've got a nasty break of your femur." He had presented such a pleasant disposition earlier that I honestly thought he was joking. When I could see he wasn't, I remarked, "I'll take the drugs now." Receiving intravenous morphine was an interesting experience. It didn't remove all my pain; rather, it induced a tranquil state in which I simply didn't care about it. I found that fascinating.

My surgeon, Hans, did a good job of putting me back together with screws, metal plates, rods, and pins. However, on my third day in the hospital, Hans wanted to push me out the door. I've learned to accept there are surgeons who get preoccupied with maintaining a nonsensically high number of operations and quick discharges.

I was too drugged up to understand the ramifications of

getting booted out of St. Vincent's. Karen threw a fit, asking the staff and nurses how she was supposed to manage my care at home by herself, pleading for sanity from everyone she was in contact with. She called her Uncle Mike (an orthopedic surgeon and department head at Scottish Rite Hospital in Atlanta) and he told her there was no way someone with my level of disability would be able to function adequately if sent home. He also said it would be impossible for Karen to deal with the dead weight I represented, raising real risks of bedsores.

There was a hospital physical therapist who had attended to me since my operation, pushing me to exercise my repaired body. When he discovered my doctor was requesting I be discharged, he also blew a gasket and left to grab a senior hospital administrator. That woman, after showing up to personally evaluate my condition and determine the necessary care protocol, decided to have me sent to a special unit at Providence Hospital in East Portland. I got transferred and spent three weeks working with therapists while being regularly evaluated by a physiatrist.

There are many poignant moments from my stay in the hospital, all of them etched in Karen's and the kids' minds, but unfortunately, not all in mine. I was heavily medicated and exhausted; I regrettably cannot recall certain events. One story often told in our family is of Ken shaving my facial growth because I was too weak and uncoordinated to do so. As he removed my stubble, Caitlin asked her mom to step outside, realizing Karen was about to burst into tears.

The stresses of the week and a half of hospital visits, and of watching her husband struggle to heal, had finally delivered Karen's first public flood of tears—on Mother's Day. The image of her son tenderly shaving his helpless father had overcome her. There were one-on-one moments with all three children during my hospital stay that I don't remember, but I'm sure they were deeply comforting to me at the time. How could they not have been?

We celebrated not just Mother's Day, but Caitlin's birthday and our anniversary in my hospital room. I missed Ken's regional track competition and his joint Eagle Scout ceremony with David Brinker (I was so proud of the boys, and relished viewing the video later). Friends from school and church banded together and provided nonstop meals for the family, shuttle services for the kids, and much more. Relatives flew in from across the country. Karen commented at the time, and has sporadically reminded me since, that sometimes we humans need hardship and misfortune to show ourselves and others the wonderful side of humanity. I agree.

My doctors and therapists assumed I would never walk again. While it would be foolhardy for me to take unaided steps today, I can do a couple of laps around the kitchen island with my walker. Those few minutes standing tall give me a totally different perspective of the world. You will often hear this from people who spend most or all their time in wheelchairs: When they can stand, for even brief moments, those glimpses of the world from *normal* height are treasured.

During the following three years, two more hip surgeries were required. The second operation removed all the hardware from the initial surgery, which had grown uncomfortable and was impairing my movements. In the third surgery, my femur was removed (the bone had died) and replaced with a titanium hip.

So, on that day I fell in 2005, the progression of my disease crashed head-on into an unexpected traumatic event. Every person with MS has a few experiences considered primary setbacks or breakthroughs. Collapsing onto concrete was a major episode in my life: It was the last day I walked or worked.

It could have been much worse. For many, it is.

CHAPTER 6
A Final Plea

Blaming God

THE YEAR 2010 had arrived. The mercury reached one hundred degrees in downtown Portland, but I disregarded that news. I obliviously left the house without my emergency beeper and cell phone. There is a direct correlation between forgetting those devices and getting myself into predicaments where said devices would have been particularly useful. You can't teach stupid.

I toggled my wheelchair to a sloping portion of our front lawn to count how many mole mounds had appeared overnight. The intense heat immediately affected my dexterity; I could feel my body growing weaker and less coordinated, but I wasn't concerned. I was comfortably seated in my chair and only seventy feet from the ramp leading into our air-conditioned home.

After counting the mounds (there were three new ones, bloody hell), I realized my body had become less able to manage the extreme temperatures than expected. My health had markedly declined since my last "getting stuck outside" episode. I hadn't factored in that my progressive disease had progressed, and I decided to move back inside. Yes, I enjoyed the sunshine, but in these conditions, ten minutes was more than sufficient.

As I spun my chair around on our slanting lawn, my body slipped forward several inches, shifting my balance just enough to make it difficult for me to sit upright and effectively operate the chair controls. I was close to sliding off completely. I surmised that if I could just get my feet planted firmly on the ground and somehow grab both armrests of my chair, I'd be able to shove off and thrust backward, settling myself into a stable position on my seat.

I prepared myself for that maneuver. Problematically, my right arm and hand, which manage the controls on the right-side armrest of my wheelchair, had already lost too much feeling to function properly (due to the heat). I then inadvertently pushed the directional toggle to the right, spinning the chair in a circle and pushing my uncoordinated body even further forward and nearly off the vinyl seat.

I was stuck in the middle of our lawn with an angry sun bearing down, without a soul in sight. There aren't many homes on our street, and their inhabitants were currently in their air-conditioned office cubicles. My pasty white skin began to bake. I grew weaker and less capable of solving my predicament.

Eventually, and for reasons I can't articulate, my mental state eroded and I traveled straight down a path of self-pity and harsh accusation. It didn't matter that I had created my problem. It didn't matter that using simple safeguards, learning from similar experiences, or doing what my wife had constantly reminded me to do, would have prevented the uncomfortable dilemma I was mired in.

My back was nearly flat on the seat of my wheelchair with my legs splayed in opposing positions. I couldn't move. My limbs had become useless attachments.

I lashed out.

Enjoying this, God? Think it's entertaining? Help me, dammit. Don't just sit there enjoying the movie. Do something. Show me that you're real.

I continued to bake. There was no breeze and the neighborhood remained still as a summer night. I grew more upset, more desperate, and more pathetic.

I don't deserve this. Help me. I swear to . . . help me! Just give me the energy to move my body.

The quiet remained; the heat bore down; the skin turned redder.

Nothing? Not a damn thing? Once again, I'm the only one getting me through this frikken disease. This is bullshit. Seriously, help, or don't ever expect anything from me. Help!

Forgotten sensations from childhood sunburns reintroduced themselves—flashbacks of enormous blisters erupting across my thighs and upper arms. I became combative, stupidly so, turning the drama into a "me and Him" confrontation.

Can't you see? Hear me? I'm burning up. Yes, I forgot my beeper and cell phone! Big deal! You think I deserve this?

That feeling of parched lips had arrived, a familiar precursor to an extended routine of Blistex lip balm.

Fine. Leave me the hell alone. You always do anyway. What have you ever done for me? Nothing. *I've got to do all this shit on my own.*

More silence and solitude.

Stress is a killer to people with multiple sclerosis. Some doctors say it isn't so (perhaps that ignorance has faded); every person with MS knows the truth. Extreme heat triggers similar complications. So on this day, I was up the creek without a paddle, barely functioning.

This is it. I'm done. Get out of my life. Or were you ever in it? Did I make you up to cope?

More heat, angst, and stress.

Watch this. You don't have a thing to do with it. I'm on my own, so don't expect an ounce of credit. Not an ounce!

Such words read as terribly immature in retrospect, but uncomfortable truths regarding my life's trials must be acknowledged. I dug deeper for some sort of solution. Misery had prompted willpower, though my demeanor remained disgraceful. My right arm had become the only appendage offering any benefit. I spent twenty minutes using any strength I had to move in tiny, excruciating increments. The left side of my body, unsurprisingly, offered nothing.

My fingers had become numb and fumbling, but I thought the bottom of my right wrist could help me. I jabbed at the controls and progressed inches at a time into the garage. I ultimately reached the ramp and door, my toes scraping upside down across the cement as the chair crept along.

My body slowly regained movement as my stress level declined and as the shade of the garage offered some sanctuary. It took me fifteen minutes to lean forward to turn the knob on the white garage door to get in the house. Once inside, I rolled toward the great room, stopped, auto-reclined, and slumbered for over two hours.

I awoke to a cool, soundless home. My shorts and shirt were no longer moist from sweat, but they remained bunched up in odd positions. Assuming I looked like a wino after a sunny afternoon passed out in a city park, I spent the next hour making myself presentable. I didn't want Karen to see me this way when she arrived home.

Healthy people might read this story and scoff with a bit of skepticism: Come on, you don't have to make your trip out to the front lawn into some *man against the elements* moment.

I understand. But the truth is there are thousands of people with illnesses like mine whose daily activities are precariously balanced; tipping the scales can deliver bad results. I was hanging out on a dock in the Caribbean a few years back, and somebody asked me how I would get to shore if I were alone and fell into the sea with my scooter. I told him there would be no problem at all; I'd just float on my back and use my right arm to propel me toward shore, then I would roll onto the sand, waiting to be discovered.

The truth is, I'd be unable to do that: I'd drown.

Anticipate. Always anticipate.

*   *   *

Truth

I began this memoir claiming optimism is my key to effectively dealing with a life encumbered by a progressive disease, but I've now presented quite a bit of personal struggle and avowed failure. Mine are candid realities, some of which may resonate with others afflicted by chronic ailments. Life isn't always easy for me. Life isn't always easy for many people, including those not dealing with autoimmune illnesses. For some, perhaps, life may never seem easy.

Here's what my extended family has had to deal with in the past few years: My beautiful niece died unexpectedly at age eighteen; my father passed away from congestive heart failure; my father-in-law died from Alzheimer's and psychosis; another niece's firstborn got diagnosed with a disease only twenty people in the world are known to suffer from; and my brother-in-law was badly burned inside a sports car that caught fire upon impact with a house.

Such difficult moments highlight an inevitability: All of us will be confronted by tragedies, illnesses, or heartbreaking circumstances. I am moved by the hope and positivity my relatives have displayed during their struggles. They are persevering, and the outlooks they're embracing are conscious pursuits.

Even when I momentarily lose my way, I know that rediscovering an upbeat demeanor is the surest path to a fulfilling life. Based on countless interactions with the healthy and the sick, it is clear to me that those who choose hopefulness are typically the most content among us.

I want to be remembered for being uplifting whether I die at sixty-five, seventy-five, or ninety-five. I would hope my family and friends might tell you the normal me, the person whose actions they've observed for decades or just a few years, typically projects hopefulness.

Remaining optimistic while battling hardships can be daunting, but I will always maintain that it's a healthy pursuit. And because I'm human, I also realize I'll disappoint myself at times, failing to embrace the very ideals I espouse.

Maintaining positivity can be elusive for myriad reasons. The trials of illness or the emotions of tragedy can certainly be factors in prompting a darker disposition. But consciously choosing to be bitter during life's difficulties would make me selfish and pathetic.

I often remind myself that a life with disease is never just about the diseased. I encounter many people, and I'm in control of my demeanor when I interact with them. I can be cheerful about my future as my body breaks down, or I can get pissed off about my circumstances and present wretchedness. It's an easy choice.

CHAPTER 7

The Gift of a Journey Companion

No one loves something or someone
more than I love you.

THERE IS ALWAYS goodness in our lives despite any problems. I never want to be the guy who constantly manages to "bring the party down" for his family and friends through a self-imposed woe-is-me temperament. When disease or hardship forces us down uncertain roads, we have opportunities to ensure these new routes are rewarding. That said, it is so much easier to make it through the morass with a positive outlook when we are fortunate enough to have a committed partner at our sides.

I probably didn't deserve to have somehow snagged Karen Busch Cruickshank; I'm not sure how much "deserving" has to do with anything we experience in life. Every day I contemplate how blessed I was to have met this wonderful woman in college, and to later share my life with her.

The athlete she fell in love with no longer exists. I hope I am still, in the more important ways a man is measured, the person she believed I would be as she considered her future with me thirty years ago. I think about these things often, because I know it is challenging to be married to a person with a progressively debilitating disease. She did not choose to spend most of her married years with a sick man; this reality was inexplicably laid in her lap one day.

While I am not yet totally reliant on Karen, I require a bit of what I'd call "regular maintenance." And my list of husbandly contributions has dwindled. I cannot drive. I cannot remove my tight compression socks from my legs. Last night I couldn't bend one of my arms to get my robe on. I can't do yardwork or housework. Sometimes I can't button my shirt (frustrating!). I drop things all over the floor (typically dark stuff on light carpet). I cannot cook meals for our guests, and I cannot help with the dishes after they leave (did I do enough of that pre-MS?). I can't put up Christmas trees and ornaments. I cannot check the oil levels of our car engines. The list of things I can't do is endless.

Karen almost never complains about the daily routine of caring for me in a much more comprehensive manner than she had ever envisioned while we were enjoying music and beer at Arizona State. I say "almost never" because it would be humanly impossible not to let this exhaustive regimen affect her occasionally. I understand: It's difficult to care for a person who has reached my level of reliance.

But she still loves me! Maybe even thinks I'm the coolest cat in the hood. (I will gladly accept just the former.) We have both come to terms with my limitations, and I am awed by her dedication to me. That beautiful woman whom I shared that first kiss with, on that diving board, at that resort, who was wearing that black dress . . . she still loves me.

Sometimes I get overwhelmed contemplating her goodness. One night recently I dwelt on how much she had accomplished that day. She had worked, shopped, gone to yoga class, cooked dinner, cleaned up after the dog, straightened up the house, grabbed wood and started a fire, made tea, and brought out dessert—all part of her regular schedule.

There she was, propped up in bed and reading as she does each work night. I considered everything she accomplishes every day, and how my life is still wonderful largely because she is wonderful. My throat tightened and I couldn't speak as she asked a question while I transferred from my chair to our bed. She put her book down and asked me what was wrong. All I could force out was, "I'm so sorry for doing this to you. I know it's hard. And unfair." She got out of bed, walked over, and hugged me.

In fishing parlance, she's a keeper.

Karen chose to return to work as a full-time art teacher after I had retired on disability, ensuring she and our children would have medical insurance coverage. When I stopped working at Intel, my family was insured during the COBRA bridge-coverage period, which would soon end. We were concerned about our insurance situation and I told myself to do some research on solutions while Karen and Caitlin were traveling.

When the primary breadwinner of an MS family reaches the point where he or she must stop working (it is important to note that most MS patients will never reach my level of debility), one of the greatest stresses is finding insurance that's affordable—or even available. Many with MS have had their family finances ruined by the medical bills incurred by the unhealthy spouse.

In our case, the challenge was exacerbated; Karen had been diagnosed with pre-cancerous atypical cell growth in her breast, which required a lumpectomy. She was prescribed a five-year treatment of Tamoxifen, a low-grade chemo medication. And then she got melanoma, which was thankfully in situ (fully contained in the first layers of skin). It was surgically removed and she was granted a clean bill of health. With her diagnoses, attaining insurance coverage would become even more difficult and more expensive.

I have access to Medicaid through my Social Security disability status, but without a more affordable solution for the family, and with some bad luck, our healthcare expenses could ultimately drain our bank accounts. Isn't it sad commentary that in the United States families *with insurance* have been bankrupted by the costs related to living with chronic illnesses?

While Karen and Caitlin were traveling, I received a call from the principal of St. Anthony School informing me she was interested in speaking with Karen about a full-time art teacher position for grades K-8 (there are only a few such positions in Portland). It honestly felt like some sort of divine intervention; I had prayed for a solution to this vexing insurance dilemma. I called Karen that evening and she, too, was excited by the prospect of lifting a huge burden from us. Then I grew concerned the school administration would proceed with filling the position before Karen had returned home.

Driving back to Portland and interviewing a few days later, I sensed Karen's disappointment as she walked through the door. She believed her conversations with school administrators had gone poorly. I first told myself it would be the school's loss if they didn't hire her; to heck with them. But my scorn was overcome by the pressing concerns of medical coverage.

Come on, I silently implored, how could they *not* offer the job to this intelligent, hardworking, and talented woman? Please, please, I pleaded from the heart, hire this remarkable lady and she'll earn the respect of the entire school.

She got the job. We got our insurance. She's an amazing teacher. Ten years later, they still love her. I knew they would.

Yes, I am blessed with a special person to share my disease

odyssey. But many of the chronically ill are less fortunate. At various times, I have belonged to Internet sites designed for people diagnosed with multiple sclerosis, where we share life experiences and discuss medical treatment options. It is also where the afflicted support those whose stories about having to "go it alone" would tear your hearts out.

So many spouses and partners become overcome with anxieties related to their futures that they exit the relationships. Sometimes they leave the MSer after months, other times after years. Of course, many never leave. I wish I could sit down with those frightened into fleeing, to try to convince them that not only do their loved ones need their support and encouragement (obviously, and more than ever), but that this life truly is just a stitch in time, and that it's noble to remain at the sick person's side. The hurdles are there, yes, but they can be cleared, and the rewards for doing so, as a companion, can be extraordinary.

Caring for someone afflicted with a chronic disease is difficult, exceptionally so at times. But these great challenges are also a test gauging who we fundamentally are as people, for the ailing and their families. Just because the road of disease isn't always a meandering journey through beautiful foothills on a sunny day, doesn't mean it won't lead us to a gratifying destination.

Admittedly, these words are coming from a sick man, not the healthy wife staring at a lifetime of sacrifice and doubt. But when I study Karen's eyes, when I listen to her speak, when I feel her love, I know my feelings are only amplifying her own.

To those who have been thrust into caregiving, don't be frightened away. Grab the hand of the person you love and tackle what lies ahead, as a team. And to my chronically ill kin, appreciate *everything* your family and friends are doing for you—they are your heroes. Stay positive, be kind, and remain hopeful. I believe it's our obligation. The key is to harmonize with each other on a level that transcends life's surprises.

Thank you, Karen, for sticking by my side. I knew you would.

To any MSer or otherwise ill person now on his own (or who always has been), I hope those you love will step up to support you. You deserve that.

CHAPTER 8

Meet My Nemesis

You "get it" when you get it.

S URE, I WISH I didn't have multiple sclerosis. Just as I wish
nobody else had MS, ALS, Parkinson's, diabetes, or any
other chronic disease. But MS is the hand I got dealt, along
with three hundred thousand other Americans.

My diagnosis came at thirty-two, which is the worldwide
average age of MS diagnosis. Until the age of twenty-two, due
to my active youth and because I was constantly working out
and growing, the effects of the disease were mostly hidden.
But I had minor symptoms that, in retrospect, I can attribute
to MS at age fourteen. These warning signs steadily advanced,
almost imperceptibly during my teens, then much more visibly
through my twenties and thirties. They are glaring today.

MS affects the ability of nerve cells in the brain and spinal
column to communicate effectively. For some reason, the body
begins to attack its own immune system, damaging the protective
myelin sheaths surrounding nerves. The resultant deterioration
leads to the scarring (lesions) people typically associate with the
disease. Fundamentally, with multiple sclerosis, the signals to
and from the brain or through the spinal canal do not reach

their intended destinations (arms, fingers, eyes, mouth, skin, legs, feet) as quickly and as clearly as they would in a healthy body. Basic movements and thoughts can become slightly or extremely difficult.

The symptoms of MS are many and varied but can include: muscle spasms, numbness, impaired balance, unsteady gait, weakness in arms and legs, fatigue, acute or chronic pain, cognitive issues, optic neuritis, poor circulation and swelling, sexual dysfunction, poor dexterity, and a host of others. Women are two to three times more likely to become afflicted than men. There is not yet a cure.

The most common form of multiple sclerosis is relapsing-remitting MS (RRMS). With this type of the disease, various symptoms will flare up, or exacerbate, before going into remission for days, weeks, months, or even years. This category afflicts approximately eighty percent of the diagnosed MS population. A person with this form of the illness could be very active and fit for varying stretches of time, then be bed-bound for a week with little or no body control. Then he might go skiing and ride bikes for months or longer with few or no symptoms. The impact on one's life can range from relatively minor to extreme.

A high percentage of those with RRMS will begin to develop some progressive disease symptoms; such people become part of the secondary progressive MS (SPMS) category of the disease. For these folks, life becomes increasingly more challenging.

I have the type categorized as primary progressive MS (PPMS), which is generally defined as a continual worsening from the time of diagnosis; thus, I have never experienced remissions or any improvement in my condition. While I hate that it never goes away, it does allow for better projection of future challenges due to its steady advance; hence, I can plan well for that inevitability. PPMS affects five to ten percent of the overall MS population.

The fourth disease form is the rarest, and is termed progressive relapsing MS (PRMS). These individuals have significant progressive neurological decline combined with occasional or regular exacerbations.

These are the four forms of multiple sclerosis each patient gets assigned to; I have provided only a cursory overview of the categories. In reality, MS can be so arbitrary that anyone diagnosed is, in fact, their own unique form. Sometimes people with MS, and others, will nonsensically debate which type is worst, or most painful, or most debilitating. My view is simple: They all stink, thank you very much.

*   *   *

Getting Afflicted

This is how I believe my disease got triggered. I have no proof for my thesis, though I have met doctors that lean toward my conclusions.

In 1973, when I was a thirteen-year-old Boy Scout, our troop traveled to the San Bernardino Mountains of Southern California for a campout. As we were hiking back out of the wilderness, I noticed the steep trail we were trekking over was full of switchbacks. Because I thought we were wasting time meandering back and forth as we descended, I took off on my own and went straight downhill, sliding on my butt or running out of control while pinballing off trees and bushes.

Upon getting to the base of the mountain, I soon began itching all over my body, particularly my face. On the drive home in the Winnebago, the irritation progressed. Soon, gorp-consuming scouts were commenting that my cheeks looked flushed. I went into the bathroom to check things out and figured it would be a good time to pee, which immediately expanded the number of body parts itching and glowing.

It wasn't long before Mom had me at a medical facility getting diagnosed with either a bad case of poison oak or poison sumac exposure. When the doctor asked whether my weenie was itching as well (in front of my mother), I lied: *No, sir.* At thirteen, the prospect of having to pull out my privates in front of Mom was rather horrifying. It still is.

News spread in the neighborhood that Ken Cruickshank had some form of alien rotting disease turning him into a brown-crusted freak day-by-day. My long-haired brothers would bring their friends over to look at their younger sibling's hideous facial infection, telling their buddies to observe "the monster." I smile at the memories.

Before I contracted whatever the heck it was, I had a face full of freckles, but after many layers of skin had peeled away over the ensuing two weeks, they were gone forever. It was rather disgusting the way the infection fully revealed itself (I will spare the ugly details). My face bore the brunt of the onslaught.

I'm convinced this episode prompted the onset of my multiple sclerosis. I believe certain people have some sort of genetic predisposition to the disease, and that a virus we all get exposed to, or an infection like the one I experienced, can trigger the demyelination of nerves in the brain and spinal nerve canal. It was within a year of this rash episode that I can clearly recall symptoms that remain visible (but much more pronounced) today.

All MS patients hold their own opinions about what causes the disease, as do neurologists and researchers. There is no consensus.

CHAPTER 9

Hello and Goodbye
to Tech

A fading sail on the horizon of life.

MY TWENTY-PLUS-YEAR CAREER certainly didn't define me in any fundamental way, but I was fortunate to have worked for some great companies with talented people. There is irony to my ending up in the high-tech industry, as I'd never studied anything related to computers in college. I get impressed by engineers that create the amazing devices whose capabilities we take for granted, but the world those bright minds inhabit seems quite foreign to me. I consider myself to have been, more than anything else, a sales and marketing guy. A businessman.

I was in Australia for part of December 1982, the same month I was to graduate from Arizona State University. An Aussie gentleman I had met in England four years earlier had flown me Down Under and offered me a cool job: representing Australian vineyards' wines to the world. He hailed from a prominent Jewish family; his father was a lord, a banking and finance leader, and a humanitarian who received a special commendation from Pope John Paul II. In the end, I decided not to take the job, but I was instantly sold on Australia; it's easy to understand why Aussies are such proud people.

Because of that trip to the land of kangaroos, I missed two of my final exams. When I approached professors about making them up, one of them told me "no problem" and the other told me "no way." The no-wayer insisted I had just accomplished something remarkably irresponsible. I looked him in the eyes, shook his hand, and told him I had enjoyed his instruction. I exited his office like an arrogant peacock, feathers raised in a blaze of colorful glory. I had a B- in the class before I had departed for Australia; the final represented forty percent of my grade; if he failed me I would not be a college graduate.

I returned to Orange County and began interviewing for jobs, telling companies I was a fresh alumnus of ASU. My final grades would have been mailed to my last address in Tempe, and I was afraid to ask ASU administrators over the phone for confirmation of my graduation status. I kept myself in the dark. One day I walked out to get the mail, nearly three months after having driven away from Arizona, and instantly recognized that a certain package was diploma-sized. I (somehow) did it! I then grew surprised that one could earn a degree from the Harvard of the Desert with a D. (To my children: Yes, Dad got a D; it's time you knew.)

For the next twenty years, I was haunted by nightmares of never having graduated from college.

Jobs were scarce in the early '80s. I was open to working in just about any industry; I only sought experience and an opportunity to advance. I never expected the process of getting a job would be easy, so I remained patient (but quietly anxiety-ridden). I played rugby in Newport Beach and softball in Huntington Beach to keep myself occupied as I continued to prospect.

A childhood friend informed one of my siblings that his fiancée was working at a tech startup in Lake Forest, California. He suggested I contact her about a possible interview. She proceeded to set me up for a round of meetings for an inside sales position. I got the job (my annual salary was a stellar $13,500!) and proceeded to begin paying off student loans; the rest was spent flying to Phoenix nearly every weekend to court Karen.

That first employer got acquired by a more prominent local computer products firm. During the organizational transition, I flirted with the idea of leaving the technology industry for a position as a sales manager for a fitness equipment manufacturer. *I'm a jock; I should sell sports stuff! Yeah, that's what I should do!* It would have been one of the dumbest decisions of my life.

Eighteen months later, I took a job within the most visible tech company in Orange County: AST Research. It was the second fastest growing company in America at the time (behind Compaq Computer).

I was twenty-six years old, had been married to this amazing woman for two years, had no idea what MS was, played sports on weeknights and weekends, and I'd just been promoted. Certainly in retrospect, life was easy and very good.

Karen and I decided to cash in on the crazy California real estate boom of the late '80s and to settle ourselves in Arizona for the long haul. I convinced my manager at AST to open a sales office in Phoenix, from where I could manage a Western US territory for the company. He obliged and I opened the branch. After it grew clear that putting an office in Phoenix had not been a prudent decision (don't let weekend warriors influence a company's sales coverage model), I was asked to move back to Orange County. Because we loved Scottsdale, I instead found a job locally, simultaneously launching my own company.

I began buying computer equipment to sell to regional businesses, but it turned out that the now twenty-eight-year-old Ken Cruickshank was too optimistic with his entrepreneurial ambitions (which sounds comedic for an industry now dominated by twenty-something tech billionaires). It wasn't difficult to grow revenues, but the expenses of supporting customers with adequate technical support, and the costs of holding physical inventory of expensive equipment, put too much of our personal money at risk. The final straw was insurance. I had bought a policy for the family but we received *terrible* claims coverage. I'm still surprised by what some health insurance companies can get away with.

A big decision loomed: pull equity out of our home to grow my business, or fold up the tent and reenter the tech mainstream that had treated us so well. To add to the decision drama, Karen was now pregnant with child number two: Caitlin.

After months of interviewing, I received job offers from Intel and Compaq Computer. A fascinating African-American man, Felix, hired me as an Intel sales representative. (Felix had been trained as an assassin by the US military and dropped into the jungles of Vietnam for some harrowing assignments. He should pen his story.)

The Cruickshanks of Arizona moved from a classic Mediterranean home in Scottsdale to a crappy bluish, squarish thing in Pleasanton, California. We loved our new town and neighborhood, but the house was a sight for sore eyes. Once a family moves out of California, even for just two years, it's difficult to buy back into the real estate enjoyed before the migration. When housing prices rise in the West, they increase disproportionately in California. It's even worse in and around Silicon Valley. Lesson learned!

We spent one year in Pleasanton before Intel moved us to Oregon, where my division was headquartered (and where we had hoped to ultimately settle). My "Intel years" lasted from 1990 until the day my drugged and MS-fatigued body collapsed onto cement in 2005.

Coincidently, Andy Grove, Intel's most famous CEO, was afflicted with Parkinson's disease (PD). His Andy Grove Charitable Foundation is helping to fund PD research for developing treatments and, one day, a cure. We are lucky to have people with his intellect, passion, influence, and resources committed to improving the lives of those struggling with debilitating chronic diseases.

My last two Intel business trips were lifestyle prognostications. I traveled to Moscow in 2001, meeting up *en route* in Germany with my work peer and neighbor. We were each seeking feedback from Russian distributors related to our groups' programs and strategies. I struggled physically while in Moscow; without my neighbor's support, I wouldn't have made it. He never asked me whether I needed help walking or carrying equipment to our meetings; he simply grabbed my briefcase or guided me up some steep cement stairs covered with snow or ice. He allowed me to maintain my at-times fragile dignity. My health had declined more quickly than my self-esteem had accepted the consequences.

We are spoiled in America; ADA laws enable people like me to get into and out of buildings and bathrooms across the country. Nothing like that exists in Russia, or, for that matter, throughout most of the world. Yes, some of this is due to the prevalence of historic structures common on other continents, but the biggest difference is mindset. In America, a person afflicted with advanced chronic disease is still generally respected and considered capable of contributing to society, and our laws dictate workplace accommodations.

About six months after that trip to Moscow, I flew unaccompanied to Mexico City for some meetings. My administrative assistant had argued against me traveling there, but I believed I could do it. The front end of the trip was fine, then I began to drag over the last thirty-six hours. By the time I had been dropped at the airport, the heat had greatly affected my ability to move. I was laboring through the terminals with my cane, briefcase, and rolling suitcase when I stopped in the middle of a congested area; I couldn't move any further. I sat on my luggage and people stared at me, wondering what the *loco gringo* was up to. Finally, a Mexican businessman walked up and asked if I needed help. I told him I did, and he assisted me through security and to my gate. That was my last business trip.

Around the time of those travels, Intel had agreed to pay for my MBA. My nightmares about not having graduated from ASU had almost completely abated, but I remained disappointed with my cavalier attitude about education during my undergraduate years. I thought that immersing myself in a program with like-minded professionals would be valuable to me and beneficial to Intel (perhaps more of the former). A good education is a wonderful asset, but it was an opportunity I'd squandered while drinking beer, fraternizing with other students, and playing rugby in the Arizona desert.

The dean of the George Fox University MBA program was hesitant about accepting me into the program, based on my Arizona State transcripts. He called and asked if I'd be amenable to discussing my admittance with a panel of decision-makers. I told him "of course" and later stated I would earn A's in every class if given the opportunity to enroll; I knew that's what I was capable of if I committed myself. They accepted me under "probation status." Earning that degree, walking across the graduation stage with my cap and gown and black shillelagh, with Karen, our children, and my program cohort in attendance, was a profound satisfaction.

As my multiple sclerosis worsened, I either volunteered

or was asked by Intel management to reduce the scope of my organization and to reallocate headcount. I was fortunate; these transitions were always done with a professional and sensitive approach; I was never blindsided and my ego was only occasionally injured. Anyone with an advanced progressive disease will have to reset expectations of their future within any employer.

Prior to my working from home in 2004, I began disappearing from the Intel campus in the afternoons to nap in my car or elsewhere—that darn MS fatigue. I have no idea if the people I worked with realized what I was doing. It was a difficult period; I felt as though I were cheating the company at times.

At age twenty-two, I can recall two distinct (non-family) achievements I had envisioned for myself by age forty-five: to be competitive in masters track meets and to be a vice president for a major corporation. Achieving those goals was never a given, though I considered their prospects reasonable and, more importantly, self-motivating.

By my mid-twenties, it was clear the track and field aspirations would never be met. By my mid-to-late thirties, I understood I would never climb the ladder of promotion to the executive ranks. These realizations evolved over time, and I had stopped struggling with their truths years before shattering my hip. It wouldn't have done any good to mope around, telling myself life was unfair. Things happen, things that are out of our control, and when they do, we own how we react to them.

There have been life phases where I've pretended to be controlling everything. As I lay in the hospital healing after my garage accident, management suggested I consider medical retirement (long-term disability). I was offended: *I will tell you and Intel when it's time for me to stop working, not vice-versa.*

What I didn't realize was that Karen had aligned with my manager; she understood I was incapable of maintaining the pace I had kept over the previous several years. Intel is an invigorating but taxing environment to work in. Struggling with advancing MS had made it difficult for me to keep my head above water. Twelve months after the accident, not yet having returned to the office, I finally decided to pursue disability retirement.

So began my new life. Followed by a few years of living in a haze.

CHAPTER 10

Finding a Path

Mining for passions can change one's life.

AFTER RETIRING ON disability at age forty-five, my broken body was healing but my MS continued progressing, and I was mentally lost. It took me years to realize it.

I grew surprised by how many work associates or friends would run into me at a party, school, or other event and comment I looked "so much better" than I had before the accident—healthier and more rested.

Managing my work and life routines had clearly taken a toll. When I engage groups of MSers to discuss the difficulties in their lives, many speak of *running on empty* as they try to fulfill their responsibilities while slowed by myriad symptoms of disease. I can relate.

What's strange is I can't present a thorough list of my thoughts during those initial months and years of rehabilitation and cerebral adjustments as a medical retiree. It's as if somebody stood before a timeline of my life, grabbed some scissors, and cut out everything from this line to that line—then tossed the wadded-up paper in the trash.

I know our kids graduated from either high school or college.

I know we celebrated holidays, birthdays, and anniversaries. I know we took trips. Ken and I attended Oregon football bowl games. I know I must have been relevant or perhaps even necessary during that stretch of time to my wife, kids, extended family, and friends (okay, maybe not *all* my friends). It's just that I don't remember the details as I would have expected.

I was living a transition one typically experiences at age sixty-five or seventy. Karen was working, the kids were getting educated, and I was wasting every minute of each day in a wheelchair. The greater that awareness became, the deeper I fell into this great chasm of nothingness. I couldn't drive or type. I was unemployed. I only went outside in the summer or early fall; the rest of the time I stayed indoors, often alone, psychologically paralyzed. Was this how it would always be? I began to wonder if four years would become fifteen, whether fifteen would become thirty. I told myself *No way.*

I concluded my problem was I had stopped dreaming.

I'd always been a dreamer! How the hell did this happen? The answer to that question didn't matter. What did matter was this: What was I going to do about it? I began searching for direction, dissecting prospects.

The obvious had already been embraced: I would never participate in my earlier life's physically active pursuits. Okay, fine, but what about the funk I was mired in? Sure, it wasn't my typical *modus operandi*, yet there I was, stuck in some sort of quagmire pulling me further into oblivion.

Deep down I knew I was capable of discovering or rediscovering something that might redefine me and my future. Something I could aspire to. Something that would motivate. For reasons I cannot explain, I just hadn't *made it happen* yet.

I had always been a storyteller and had made comments over the previous twenty years about possibly writing a book. What did I know about creating a compelling written story?

Not much, but I told myself I could learn or, at least, I could try. I had enjoyed writing analyses for case studies during my MBA program. I had written poems when I was young (including a colorful one about a bully classmate that got *me* suspended from school for three days). Could I learn enough to tackle writing a four-hundred-page book?

After graduating from Arizona State, I didn't read very much. When I did flip through pages, they were typically bound within the covers of a nonfiction book or tech industry magazine. I had finished one work of fiction since 1981, *The Zero Factor* (William Oscar Johnson). When I was in the hospital in 2005, a friend since childhood, Paul, sent me three paperbacks to consume: *Pale Horse Coming* (Stephen Hunter), *Plum Island* (Nelson DeMille), and *Trevayne* (Robert Ludlum). The books sat on my bedside for ten days before I had even read the covers.

Soon thereafter, twenty pages into *Pale Horse Coming* (an ultimate guys' book), I was hooked. Two weeks later, I had chewed through all three paperbacks. Then I read five more. Then ten. I shot over thirty books and I just kept reading: Hemingway, London, Thompson, Child, King, Berry, Patterson, and many others. Karen had previously been telling me about some guy named Ken Follett; she'd been trying to get me to devour even one of his bestsellers for years. She continued advocating: "I think you'll really like his historical fiction and thrillers."

Having ultimately taken the bait, I annoyed her immensely by exclaiming how great *Pillars of the Earth* and *Night Over Water* were. She replied, "Enough! You're acting as if you discovered Ken Follett. I did, a long time ago. Not you." Oh well.

Karen was also correct about something more important: My path through the haze of a lack of purpose was staring me in the face. It all began to make sense: *I needed to pursue the craft of writing.*

How would I get started? What was the right approach? I was presently hooked on fiction, but what about my decades-old preference for nonfiction? Should I shelve it? Even though I'd always enjoyed reading biographies and memoirs?

Driving up Highway 101 many summers earlier, I had once commented to Karen about how I envisioned a Spanish galleon moored off the Oregon Coast, and conquistadors burying their Aztec bounty inside sandstone caverns carved by millennia of westerly breezes. I had also been contemplating my once very active life and the many ways in which it had become so profoundly altered by my eventual diagnosis and progression of MS.

That was the moment of inspiration: *Two book ideas!* Now I simply needed to update my speech-to-text software and begin "typing." My writing adventure would soon commence. I was super excited.

It took me two years to write two pages.

* * *

Years later, writing has literally changed my life. I do it every day. Anticipate it. Enjoy it. And when I have the energy: *I must simply write.* I feel as if I have forced myself to complete a Masters in Writing through my efforts. I'm no Hemingway, but I'm one heck of a lot closer than I was five years ago.

The beauty of this passion for the written word is that every day is now an adventure. I travel wherever I want to go. Meet people who exist only in my mind. Say or do anything I want! I'm learning new things, developing my skills, and getting closer to the ultimate end point: producing a library of completed stories and books. I often contemplate those words, because I feel it's an incredibly cool and empowering thing to do: *create something out of nothing.*

Some have stated that becoming a successful fiction writer

requires imagination, stubbornness, and technical writing skills. When I began my great adventure of storytelling, I felt I possessed the first two qualities in abundance. I am forcing myself to conquer the third, while realizing that fully mastering the skills of writing is likely an unattainable goal, for anyone.

I began creating my psychological thriller, *The Barn*, before I had read a single sentence regarding the craft of writing. Yes, it took me two years to pen a few paragraphs, but one day I confronted myself: *Get after it, Ken!* I wrote over twenty pages in ten hours. That was the breakthrough; the dam had been obliterated. Since then, I've never been unable to scribe something when the mood strikes (which it does often). That's not to say I write something *impressive* every time I strap on my headset, only that I can pound out sentences whenever I want to.

Weeks after beginning my psychological thriller, I started the memoir you are presently reading. It has been a deeply personal and cathartic story to write. If you're still turning the pages, then perhaps I've figured out how to effectively present some thoughts.

Writing is not easy. At least, it hasn't been for me. I have rewritten The Barn twenty-four times, line by line, beginning to end. I never wrote an outline that could have served as a guide for writing the four hundred-page work of fiction; I just unleashed my imagination and jotted down whatever popped into my mind. This might not be the way I'll write future books, but it was the best way to complete my first two manuscripts. It made the process of editing so laborious, so very slow and excruciating, that it was inevitable I'd gain volumes of knowledge as I fixed (and continue fixing) broken sentences, paragraphs, and chapters. It's difficult. I love it.

After I had established a writing groove, the days flashed by. Just as business had once become my "sport" after my disease had advanced in my twenties and thirties, writing has similarly supplanted business as my primary ambition.

Any disease-afflicted (or healthy) person can reinvent himself and give his life more dimension if he truly commits to that end. It may not happen quickly, it may not happen easily, but it will happen. And it could be magical.

For several years, I sensed certain friends or family members were hesitant to accept that my interests in writing books could sufficiently fulfill me. I perceive no doubts in their expressions today. They are thrilled that my commitment to telling stories is genuine, unwavering. No one will ever wonder what I do with my spare time again.

Because I have none.

I'm an author. It feels good.

PART II
A Youth Unfettered

If you don't know my past,
you can't understand my future.

CHAPTER 11
Bloodlines

"Shake the hand that shook the hand of John L. Sullivan."
—Grandpa Kenny

I FEEL BLESSED HAVING grown up in a large, active, and spirited family in what I believe was one of the most beautiful parts of the world during the 1960s and early '70s: Orange County, California. Wide-open land with rolling hills of lemon, orange, and avocado groves, sunny blue skies for most of the year, migrating Monarch butterflies, the smell of wonderful indigenous flora in the foothills, and those towering eucalyptus trees I just assumed had been growing in California for millennia (I learned they were imported from Australia). My hometown of Tustin was defined by hardworking people, big families, excellent schools, and uncrowded streets. Mom and Dad settled us there in the early '60s.

My maternal grandparents emigrated separately from Galway, Ireland, to New York City in 1923 (grandmother) and 1924 (grandfather). My grandmother, Celia, contracted typhoid fever in New York City, which coincided with a regional epidemic traced back to an Irish woman named Mary, who became famously demonized as "Typhoid Mary." Celia's uncle, a successful businessman in California, offered to pay for her move west, believing the dry, warm air would boost her health (he was right; she lived to reach one hundred). An Irishman who was clearly smitten followed the same route west (*go, Grandpa, go!*), initially stating he intended to stay in LA for just a short period. The rest, as we say, is history: John Kenny married Celia McLoughlin in 1928, in Southgate, California.

An interesting side note on my grandmother's uncle is that he owned three prime-location service stations in the LA area. One of them was placed halfway between Long Beach and Los Angeles, and it served as a combination gas station, mechanic shop, and lunch center. He was offered close to $100,000 (a huge sum in 1929) for that single location by Standard Oil Company, an offer he turned down because, "If it's worth that much to them, then it's worth even more to me." Sadly, the Depression hit and he got wiped out financially. But before losing everything he had gained a reputation as a "good man," allowing many of his patrons to buy gas on account so they could drive around Southern California seeking employment. When he died several years after the Depression, there were records of names and dates for considerable "gas loans" that had accumulated but had never been repaid.

Dad's ancestors departed Scotland in the 1850s, settling first in Canada, then in Omaha, Nebraska, for a stretch, and ultimately reaching Glendale, California, in 1922. Family legend has it that one of the Cruickshanks earned the first liquor license in dry Omaha (*darn those Catholics!*).

Another long-standing piece of family lore is this story: In 1905, John Cruickshank, my great-grandfather's brother, left a Nebraska bar one evening and galloped home over rolling hills dotted with massive trees. Unfortunately, the story went, one of those oaks had a limb extending horizontally at the same height as John Cruickshank's head. He died instantly by the impact (to which I'd advise, don't drink and ride). It turns out the story is inaccurate. My brother Bob did some research and discovered the following article regarding John D. Cruickshank's actual demise, which was published in the *Nebraska State News*:

FOUND DEAD UNDER HIS WAGON: Farmer Is Killed in Accident Which No One Sees

Fremont—John Cruickshank of Union Township was killed by being thrown from a wagon while driving to his home in North Bend. His body was found under the wagon box at the side of the road about four miles north of North Bend. The horses had freed themselves and were standing nearby. How the accident occurred no one knows.

I'm not sure which story is more intriguing, the lore or the truth.

My mother, Margaret, was the oldest of three daughters born to Celia and John Kenny. My father, Richard, was the middle of three boys born to Arthur and Frances Cruickshank. At age twenty, my beautiful mom walked across the stage during her employer Ducommun's holiday production, with her black hair, porcelain skin, and blue eyes. My future father attended the play, and he asked a buddy who worked with Mom, "Who's that?" The friend replied, "Oh, that's Margaret Kenny. She's a nice girl." Dad responded, "Well, I'm a nice guy."

Richard (Dick) and Margaret married in 1951 and ended up rearing ten Cruickshanks born over a twelve-and-a-half-year span. Five boys and five girls: Cecelia, Rich, Beth, John, Bob, Ken, Fran, Peg, Jim, and Cathy. Five children with light brown or blond hair, and five with brunette or black hair. Six with blue eyes and four with brown or hazel eyes. Ranging in height from five-seven to six-four. I am child number six, Kenneth Francis Cruickshank, self-proclaimed "oldest of the second five." I stand

six-two (when holding my walker) with blue eyes and a head of
hair that grayed too early.

Mom

Margaret achieved something remarkable—*she* raised ten
Cruickshanks. I say this because Dad was a captain for Trans
World Airlines (TWA) during the heyday of the airline industry,
from the 1950s through 1980. Back then, pilots were absent
from home more days per year than they are today. Hence,
Mom took control of the clan while flying solo: disciplining,
guiding, cooking, cleaning, laundering, transporting, shopping,
holiday decorating, sewing, volunteering, meeting with teachers
or principals, coordinating doctor and dentist visits, and a host
of other unique and challenging responsibilities.

We Cruickshanks have been privileged to have a mother who
is intelligent, multitalented, and totally committed to doing the
best job she could at raising us kids—as her husband circled the
globe over and over and over. It is my unyielding opinion that
most mothers would not have been able to manage or cope with
the demands of raising the Cruickshank Clan.

Margaret was (and is) a fiercely independent woman. At
age fifteen, she and her mother visited a convent whose nuns
were hoping to provide Mom a quality education at a Catholic
college prep school in Ohio, two thousand miles away. The
mother superior they met with in Southern California appeared
excited by the prospects of offering a capable young woman a
life-altering opportunity. In fact, they remarked, Mom's trunk
had already been packed for the journey east.

While the nuns never stated as much, my mother thought she
might find herself in a strange place, surrounded by religious
zealots whose ultimate ambition might be to turn her into a
nun—and that was *not* the vocation she had envisioned for

herself. She suggested the trunk be promptly unpacked. I smile when I think of her making her position exceedingly clear.

Margaret later transitioned from the exciting life of a young woman in Los Angeles after WWII to what must've been the mind-numbing reality of raising her ten children. She insists she has been fulfilled through her lifetime of trials and joys associated with heading our vibrant family. I believe she was destined for her role; her legacy is a great network of children, grandchildren, and great-grandchildren.

Mom helped instill morals, a strong work ethic, goals orientation, and faith. She guided us with an enduring belief we could succeed in life, and that any failures were always just temporary. She gave everything she had to raise her family. She deserves great respect and good fortune.

El Supremo

Dad's plane was riddled with bullets and flak covered the skies as he bombed the Japanese on the island of Formosa (modern-day Taiwan). He accepted that there was a good chance his Jolly Rogers B-24 Liberator would not make it back to base, that it might crash and burn like so many other aircraft had in the South Pacific and European battle theaters. One of the pilots in his squadron had also flown missions over Europe, and he informed the crew that there was more antiaircraft fire over Formosa than over any German target he'd bombed. So, Dad prayed from the cockpit; the entire crew was praying out loud, leaning on whatever faiths they had been raised in, pleading to make it back to their loved ones. Dad promised Mother Mary he'd wed a good Catholic girl and bring six children into the world if he survived. The Liberator limped back to Biak Island, and he obviously made good on his commitment.

Most of my friends remember my dad, who enigmatically

adopted the moniker *El Supremo* for himself, as a car junkie and mechanic-hobbyist who always had a cigar in his mouth and who would call each of my buddies "Tiger"—because there were too many kids around to keep their names straight. Occasionally, Dad would appear with a Band-Aid taped around his stogie, after it had gotten bent as he laid on his back doing car repairs. He was a tall, lean man who I always thought resembled an SS officer: stern gaze, prominent nose, black hair, and an imposing presence. But that image was at odds with a man who possessed a keen sense of humor and a penchant for fun and adventures.

Dad was that rare person whose career involved his life's greatest passion: flying. If he wasn't in the left seat of an L-1011 or 747, he'd often be enjoying the local skies in one of the Piper Cherokee or Bonanza aircraft he owned during his lifetime. Though he was a bomber pilot in WWII, as a kid I thought he should have been a P-51 Mustang ace. I remember flying with him over the ocean, where he would dive-bomb from the skies to look at migrating gray whales off the shores of Newport Beach, or fly thirty feet above the swells, giving me the rush sensation of seawater flashing by at high-speed.

My father had a particular interest in Chrysler 300s from the late 1950s. His favorite was "The Bomb," an appropriate moniker for a 1957 Chrysler 300 C sporting a massive Hemi engine that roared like no other car on the road. He enjoyed driving The Bomb fast, often too fast, and that tendency was ingrained in all his sons. Like so many other American men my age, I wish those autos of yesteryear Dad had once owned were still in our family; they were true classics.

El Supremo left us in 2011. My mother carries on as matriarch of the Cruickshank Clan. She may outlive us all.

Ireland and the UK have two of the highest incidences of MS per capita in the world. I am essentially Scottish-Irish, with some German (which also has a higher-than-average MS incidence). Neither of my parents was stricken with multiple sclerosis, though Mom and one sister have developed rheumatoid arthritis (RA), another autoimmune disease. None of my brothers or sisters has MS.

Were Mom, my sister Beth, and I randomly afflicted by our diseases? How much of a role did genetic predisposition play? I hope that cures will one day make these moot contemplations, for all of us.

CHAPTER 12

Country Lane

"My mom says you have too many kids in your family."
—Redhill Elementary schoolmate

PEOPLE SOMETIMES REMARK "life is short, enjoy it," and, "life is an adventure, go conquer." I fully buy into these perspectives and hope I always will. Margaret constantly told her ten children "there is nothing in life you cannot accomplish." It's a perspective that numbs difficulties and enables a positive outlook while dreaming about the future. So, I was a kid who participated in all the havoc a neighborhood full of mischievous youths could create and who, at the same time, was always fantasizing about the exciting things he could do, and would do, when he "grew up."

As an adolescent in Tustin, California, I stayed out all day, getting involved in every sort of sport and mischief imaginable. On our street with fifty-plus children dispersed among just twelve houses, there was a heck of a lot of misbehavior to be had—and we all had quite a bit of it. All I can do is beam at the recollections.

All the young children on our street named Country Lane would walk to school in the '60s and '70s, unlike today, where school parking lots are sometimes congested with SUVs dropping off kids who live two blocks away. We would travel in packs to Redhill Elementary, or ride bikes and cars to Hewes Junior High and Foothill High.

I hold fond memories of my schooling experiences. I always tell people I must have been given an excellent early education because once I left Redhill Elementary I honestly didn't do a lot of studying in junior high, high school, or even college. That's not meant to be a stupidly inaccurate quip, nor is it a boast—it's simply the truth. The public school system in California back then was outstanding, a far cry from its (generally) lagging ranking today. I was a beneficiary of that system. I didn't push myself again as a student until I earned my MBA over twenty years later.

I can rattle off most of the names of my teachers from Redhill Elementary, and I cheerfully recall those who had a profound effect on developing me as a student: Mrs. Boss, Mrs. Groendyke, Mrs. Adair, and Mrs. Glass. Most of them have surely graduated to that great school in the sky by now, but I tip my imaginary hat in their directions: Thank you for your focus, skills, and patience.

As teens, the young men on our street would partake in activities you'd be put in jail for today, perhaps even shot for. Some of the teenagers of Country Lane once poured gasoline into a manhole placed in the middle of our cul-de-sac. They rigged a fuse that could be lit from a distance but that would eventually fall through the holes on top of the seventy-pound metal cover. When the fuse floated down the shaft, it ignited the gasoline at the bottom of the well. *Kaboom!* The explosion could be heard a mile away as the steel lid blew ten feet into the air. People came running out of their homes assuming something dreadful had just occurred, but grew relieved (and I am sure mad as hell) to find it was just another neighborhood boys' experiment.

In seventh grade, David Rusk and I were attempting to build rockets out of boring legal fireworks. We got creative and strapped stationary cylindrical fountains onto a two-foot-long piece of light balsa wood. We grinned as we lit our homemade missile from the street and watched it take to the skies. We had perfectly calculated its flight path out of the tube serving as a launchpad. It was glorious witnessing our creation fly through the air and away from the neighborhood. It was inglorious watching the projectile do a half loop and come screaming back toward the empty lot we were standing next to: a one-acre lot full of dead and highly combustible two-foot-tall midsummer weeds. We were doomed.

Moments after the rocket had landed in the tall brush, flames exploded from the field. This was the second time I had accidentally set the lot ablaze, though it was clear to me this was a much more serious incendiary situation than the first episode.

I will never forget the image of my poor mother running barefoot across the street in a blue skirt and white blouse, carrying a hose she hoped would control the blaze. Of course, the water from a single line would not be sufficient to slow the advance of this roaring inferno. We were fortunate; so much dark smoke had billowed into the sky that the Tustin Fire Department had quickly assessed the emergency and arrived in time to save the surrounding homes.

My punishment? The firemen gave me a lecture on the dangers of fireworks before letting me check out the cabin in one of the cool fire trucks that had raced to save the day. That was the less harried and less damning world I lived in during the '70s. Though I will admit, a bit more punishment from the brave professionals would have been appropriate. (I should add that, when Captain Dick returned home from his latest globe-hopping, he was significantly more upset than the firemen.)

I have always relished any kind of sporting activity. At age fourteen, I was still a scrawny kid. A neighbor, we called him Mr. Olympia, suggested I come into his garage for an assessment of my strength and tips on building up my body. He was a physical education teacher with a barrel chest, massive limbs, and a neck one typically sees on Texas Longhorns. He had been recruited to play football at USC but injuries ruined his dream.

When Mr. Olympia asked me if I thought I could bench press 110 pounds, I immediately responded, "Of course!" So I lay down on the bench, ready to prove just how darn strong Kenny Cruickshank was. He stood over me and asked if I had a firm grip on the bar he was holding in his sturdy hands; I told him I was ready and he let go. When I lowered the bar to my chest I couldn't budge it upward. I was devastated, knowing it just wasn't very much weight. I waited for his judgment and ridicule but heard nothing of the sort. He pulled some iron plates off the bar and suggested we start with eighty pounds. His gentle reaction to my great disappointment was never forgotten. Lifting weights and building up my body eventually became a great boost to my self-esteem, a tonic for any insecurities.

Reflecting on my active youth of tag, kickball, baseball, basketball, football, ding-dong ditch, kick the can, BB guns, lawn darts, Cox airplanes, building forts, digging tunnels, throwing eggs and oranges at school buses, lighting cherry bombs and M80s, or any other manner of sport and dereliction, I cannot think back to a single moment where someone would have grown concerned about my well-being. I was full of life and appeared super healthy, enjoying a fantastic childhood seemingly unencumbered by any illness.

And yet, at some point during that fabulous youth, I was

touched by the invisible hand of the progressive disease that affects nearly every aspect of my life today.

The first visual manifestation of multiple sclerosis appeared a year or two after I had begun lifting weights regularly. I noticed during the bench and incline presses that my left arm would lag the full extension of my right arm. The more repetitions I completed, the more energy I exerted, the faster my heart would beat, the greater the lag of the left arm would become. At the time, I assumed my right arm and shoulder were simply stronger than the left side. In retrospect, this was certainly a glimpse of the progression of my MS.

That darn left side of my body has withered significantly as the years have ticked by.

CHAPTER 13
Clan Cruickshank

It all seemed pretty normal back then.

After rolling one of our family's Fiat 600s at age fifteen, I continued to log time driving various vehicles whenever my older siblings and parents were not around. It was no surprise to me when, at age sixteen, I scored one hundred percent on both the written and driving exams required to earn my license. I don't know how many prospective motorists earn such scores on their first attempts, but if my driving record is any testament, the fewer that do, the better.

Having earned those flawless scores, I proceeded to get into seven accidents in just over two years. I was that insane teenage race car driver parents shuddered to contemplate. Too fast was never fast enough. My brain had clearly not fully developed; obvious dangers were trivial impediments. As surprising as the number of fender-benders was, perhaps an even greater wonder was that only one of the accidents was ever reported by the police, and none of them affected my insurance.

My first set of family wheels as a legitimate motorist was a red 1970 Volkswagen Beetle, known among my high school buddies as the T3, a nod to its blue and yellow California license plate that read TEE333. I hold great memories of the classic car, including playing "tag" on Skyline Drive in the hills of North Tustin, where Good Buddy Ron and I lived. Ron would commandeer his father's huge black Lincoln Continental Town Car and attempt to tag my Volkswagen's rear bumper with his car's front bumper, and vice versa. In retrospect, considering the speed and mass differentials, I remain thankful he didn't tap me off the hillsides.

For many young men, cars and girls are inexorably bound together. I was no exception. Prior to reaching the legal driving age, I was disappointingly insecure about mingling with the opposite sex. Carol Vanderpool was beautiful and sweet, and all my male classmates at Redhill Elementary dreamed of holding her hand. Just as my interest in her goddessness was peaking in fifth grade, Peter Bender asked me to meet him after school one day—so I could witness him kissing pretty Carol. My heart was broken. In sixth grade, I dreamed about Jule Schiffelbein, but I was never privileged enough to clutch her hand, either. In eighth grade, I was sure that Laura Curnutt liked me, but then Steve Arnold (RIP) swept her off her feet and I got designated as roadkill. I certainly appreciated a nice young lady as much as anyone else; I just didn't have the nerves to interact with them the way I desperately wanted to.

In high school, I convinced myself that driving a really cool car might lead to breaking through the ice separating me from all the lassies. I worked at McDonald's and Knott's Berry Farm to save money for impressive wheels and found the car of my dreams for sale on the side of a road in Tustin: a black-on-black 1970 Dodge Challenger 383 Magnum SE. Dad loaned me the extra cash necessary to acquire the muscle car. Girls were bound to dig me. All of them.

Sadly, the car never did become the chick magnet I had hoped for. But that was okay, because hanging out with Ron,

Steve, Al, and George was a fine experience, too. We would often meet at Dick Naugle's for burritos around nine during the week, and at midnight on the weekends. Ron and I would arrive in my Challenger, Steve would show up in his Buick GS with its 455 engine, and George would show up in his father's big block "Toro Pig" Grand Torino. We would roll down our windows and press our biceps against door panels to exaggerate our physical magnificence, or lean up against the cars in parking lots, hoping a bevy of beautiful girls would show up (they never did), while listening to the Beatles, Zep, the Who, Van Halen, Aerosmith, Styx, Boston, and Foreigner. Man, life was good.

One night, as Good Buddy Ron and I were returning home from a friend's house, I opened up my Challenger to 107 miles per hour on 17th Street—I clearly remember looking at the speedometer. I reminded myself that a mile ahead there was a prominent bump in the road, on top of which lay some railroad tracks. *Everyone* knew to slow down to about forty before passing over the rise (which has since been smoothed out), but I figured, what the heck, let's meet that launch pad at 107 miles per hour. No one was on the road in either direction. It was a good time to test the laws of aerodynamics.

There is a memory etched in both of our minds, of my muscle car bottoming out hard on the upward slope, with the sounds of scraping metal and images of sparks streaming out from both sides of the chassis, getting sprung airborne into *no man's land*, and the car leaning slightly to the left as we literally flew. No words were exchanged; the situation required my absolute focus for reentry. I believe Ron's sole contemplation regarded getting him home safely (to change his boxers, perhaps).

We lived, but what a stupid, stupid thing for me to attempt. Regardless, my buddies and I continued to drag race on side streets or on the highways late at night. Good Buddy Ron was uncomfortable driving on tall bridges, so I made sure to drive on tall bridges at high speeds whenever we were in Long Beach, steel pillars flashing by his passenger window, inches from his face. *Fast and Furious,* they'd call it today.

The most serious, and ironic, misfortune related to my driving escapades was when I crashed one of Ron's father's company trucks into a US Postal Service mail truck—as I was racing to the post office to complete the round-trip in half the time of others, on a bet. Fortunately, no one was injured during any of my car-related antics.

The streets of Tustin were filled with classic cars in the '70s: Cudas, Challengers, Olds 442s, Mustangs, GTOs, GTXs, Daytonas, Z28s, and on and on. These legendary appellations mean nothing to Karen (she mockingly refers to them as "high schoolers' cars"), but to my buddies and the few female gearheads appreciating metal works of art, these autos exemplified our era and are fondly reminisced about. If we had all kept the cars we owned as zit-faced teenagers, many of our pending retirements would look much brighter today. A missed opportunity.

My driving irresponsibility was, unfortunately, transferable to winged aircraft. When I was eighteen and attending classes at Orange Coast College in Costa Mesa, I decided to get formally trained to earn my private pilot's license. Similar to acing my written and driving tests to get my driver's license, I already knew how to inspect, fire up, taxi, take off, fly, and land an airplane; I had flown with Captain Dick many times over the skies of Southern California. The flight instructor I was paying quickly realized I was proficient.

I soloed (considered capable of flying by myself) after just a few hours of lessons. I then proceeded to attempt something incredibly daft, with no one else aboard. In 1978, it was not required that a flight instructor demonstrate how to regain control of a plane stuck in a downward spiral, one of the *worst-case scenarios* a pilot might encounter. While my instructor chose not to show me the stall and spin situation, he verbally communicated the steps necessary to regain control if I ever found myself in such a quandary. I was quietly disappointed with not being able to experience the thrill of an airplane spinning in tight circles toward earth.

Later, I rented a Cessna from Shaw Aviation and lifted off from John Wayne Airport in Orange County, which is (surprisingly) one of the busiest airports in the United States. Anticipating the thrill of an unadvised maneuver, I ascended thousands of feet above the waters just beyond Newport Beach, and then I pulled back on the wheel, listened to the stall indicator "buzz" its warning, felt a sudden drop and weightlessness, pushed the rudder, and began spiraling downward. All I saw out my cockpit window were the sun-tinged blue seas turning round and round. My heart began beating more loudly, but I knew all I had to do was employ the steps my instructor had verbalized.

Due to youthful exuberance, I was too aggressive with my recovery actions. I overcorrected and pushed the plane into a spin in the opposite direction. It's one thing to cope with a *planned* emergency, quite another to react to something *totally unanticipated*. I recalled my dad previously telling me that the wings of some aircraft had been snapped off during spins because of too much speed and poorly executed recoveries. It didn't matter that I had never heard of that happening to a Cessna 150; I suddenly envisioned my fuselage becoming a torpedo headed for water that, at a certain speed, would deliver the equivalent of slamming into cement. Dead silence is another memory.

Stay calm, I kept repeating, stay calm. I performed the recovery procedures with more urgency, and perhaps more than a slight sense of dread. *Pull back on the throttle. Opposite rudder. Stop the spinning. Regain control. Yoke forward.* It worked (and it was the last spin and recovery I ever performed).

*   *   *

I clearly thought I was immortal as a teen, but that's a common view for young men, isn't it? I hadn't yet been exposed to tragedies or death. My mom's parents were still alive. My dad's father had died before I was born, but Grandma Cruickshank was still playing the piano beautifully in her nineties. My older brother Bob had nearly died at age seven after falling through shower glass, but I barely remembered anything about the accident (a neighbor had rushed Bob and Mom to the hospital in his new 427 Vette, saving Bob's life). My brother John wouldn't die for four more years. In my mind, *everyone* was immortal in the late '70s.

It's probably good for teenagers to remain unaffected by deep thoughts of mortality, to be oblivious to some of the inevitabilities and arbitrary misfortunes of life. That said, I delivered countless lectures to my own children regarding anything presenting even remote risks of harm to them or their futures. It is strange that a father so unencumbered by fear of accidents or the finitude of our time on earth during his own youth would burden his children with such (excessive?) safeguarding.

Stripping away the veneers of adolescent naïveté, I realize that the '70s were not always as innocent and carefree as they seemed at the time. As a typical teenager, I stayed focused on me and my buddies, and much less so on the dramas playing out around me. Writing these pages has challenged me to recall events within my family that must have been terribly difficult episodes for my siblings and parents.

One evening, after receiving a disturbing phone call from a young woman we knew, Mom and Bob rushed out of the house. When they arrived at the girl's home, she was frantically screaming. Bob was the first person (even before the young lady) to find the girl's father dead from putting the barrel of a shotgun into his mouth and blowing the back of his head off. My heart breaks for Bob, my mother, and for the sweet girl who became fatherless that night. No one should ever have to confront such madness. My brother Rich arrived at the scene later—it was his girlfriend's father who had taken his life. Rich removed some remnants of the man's head from the roof of the home after the coroners had departed.

At age twenty, my sister Cecilia left for a vacation in Africa with her best girlfriend. Imagine two blondes with backpacks trekking over dirt roads across Western Africa, with no men accompanying them. The idea of it sounds so patently ludicrous today that it might read like I'm making it up. Two years after her journey, I asked Cecilia where she had gotten a cool wooden chair, which had clearly been carved by hand. "From an African chief," she replied nonchalantly. Obviously, her great adventure had become a faded memory, absent any contemplation of its dangers.

My brother John was working at a gas station in 1979. A drug-crazed man with a pistol advanced, led him to the cash register, and put the barrel of the gun to his head, demanding money. My brother thought he was going to die. It wasn't until after John's death from an auto accident, in 1981, that I learned how the event had affected his psyche. I sometimes ponder the anxieties John must have grappled with when reliving the event.

When he was twenty, my brother Rich apparently needed a respite from the good life in Orange County. He grabbed his TWA flight pass and began globe-hopping, eventually ending up on a kibbutz in Israel. He had been gone for three months, and my father had been unable to find any information on his whereabouts for two of those months. I have strong memories of sensing sadness for my mother at the time; had she silently accepted that something tragic had happened to her oldest son? What we didn't know was that his Israeli friends on the kibbutz had recommended he fly back to America—the Yom Kippur War had broken out (1973). Our family was sitting at the dining table when Rich returned home. He walked in, nodded to all of us, said "hey," strolled into the kitchen, and poured himself a glass of milk. The sounds of my mother's relief remain embedded in my mind.

I realize my family's dramatic experiences were unique, not attributable to living in a different time. I've read articles and seen statistics suggesting the '70s were safer than today, and other data drawing exactly the opposite conclusions. I do know we all used to walk to school as children, without hesitations. Many of us were Boy Scouts, Girl Scouts, Little Leaguers, and altar boys—great experiences devoid of any unsettling considerations. Of course, the darker side of humanity—adults with bad intentions targeting the most vulnerable among us—certainly existed.

The world only *seemed* totally safe back then.

Regardless of any hindsight resulting from today's broader societal awareness of myriad lurking dangers, I can't help measuring my teenage years as mostly special. I recall wreaking havoc in Tustin and traveling solo and I grin broadly. And though my MS has worsened, tragedies have taken place, and people I've known and loved have passed away, every day the sun rises and I'm hopeful of the future. Just as I was during my youth.

CHAPTER 14

Fear and Flight

Run, Ken, run!

DESPITE THE GENERALLY upbeat recollections of my adolescence, there's one experience I'm forced to acknowledge was disturbing. It highlights my obliviousness and naïveté at age seventeen.

After years of traveling with our father or family throughout the world, some of us ten Cruickshanks started venturing out on our own. We independently explored parts of Europe, Africa, the Middle East, and Asia. As the offspring of a TWA pilot, we could fly for free anywhere the airline flew, if there were non-revenue seats available. Thankfully, there were almost always vacant seats.

1977

As a teen, my favorite place to fly to alone was England. I loved London and the beauty and quaintness of the villages dotting the countryside, and cute English girls with those wonderful accents were intoxicating. I would hop off the plane at Heathrow

Airport with forty or fifty bucks in my pocket, excitedly anticipating whatever lay ahead.

On this journey, I met a smartly dressed Jamaican man near Hyde Park, also named Ken, who seemed well-informed about England's current events and the London music scene (is there any sound better than English rock?). He was probably eight to ten years older than me, exceedingly proper, and wore a finely-tailored business suit.

Ken the Jamaican helped me plan what I hoped would be a few great days of traveling solo through the countryside. He then suggested a great pub down the street, where we enjoyed a fish and chips meal while I formulated travel logistics.

Jamaican Ken learned that my typical routine was to show up in town without a place to stay or enough money for a decent hotel, so he offered me a bed for my first evening, in an extra room at his flat. At that point in my life, there was nothing prompting me to pause at his offer for any reason; I felt safe and confident in my surroundings. I thanked him and accepted his invitation, after which we caught a cab to his residence.

His flat was exceptionally clean but unremarkable in every other way. We chatted for quite a while as he prepared a meal for dinner. I was considering how lucky I was to have scored not only a free place to crash, but also a *gratis* home-cooked meal. After dinner, we sipped on some English black tea with sugar and cream, just as I would have at Grandma Kenny's in Laguna Beach. Then I headed to bed.

At some point in the evening, my deep slumber weakened and I realized somebody was standing over me. In a shocking moment, I glanced up to see Ken the Jamaican peering at me while fully undressed. In a quiet voice, he asked me if I wanted to do something that stunned me.

I was just seventeen years old and had grown up in a conservative home and sheltered environment—this was a confusing development for me. After appraising the situation for seconds, I concluded that a) I was far outside my element and b) it was likely unsafe. The truth is, I was terrified.

Thanks to Country Lane's weightlifting coach, I had been on a workout regimen for over three years. While I still wasn't very big as a high school senior, I'd grown deceptively strong. The only solution I could think of required every developed muscle in my upper body. Without saying a word, I moved to the side of the bed and slowly rose as my adrenaline was exploding throughout my body. I stood up and Ken the Jamaican gave me a look that still confounds me.

My father had instructed us boys to always "take the first shot" if we ever found ourselves in a situation that was definitely going to end in fisticuffs (and that was my anxious conclusion, right or wrong, after moments of evaluation). I counted one, two, three—then *Bam!* I hit him as hard as I could in the solar plexus.

The air left his body and he bent over in pain. I delivered the second blow with even greater force. I learned at that moment how adrenaline can infuse a person with great strength and quickness. He made a grunting sound and fell to the ground. It wasn't Hollywood; it was frightfully real.

I was standing in my tighty whiteys next to a crumpled, naked man in a foreign country, scared and battling the urge to hysterically panic. I grabbed my belongings and duffel bag and broke for the door, which had three chain locks and one bolt lock securing it. Pulling the chain locks from the doorjamb was not difficult, but I struggled with simply turning the dead bolt because I anticipated a knife being stuck in my back, or a cord being placed around my neck. I was screaming "no, no, no!" as I twisted the knob back and forth. I was finally able to open the door and I ran outside like the spooked animal I was.

Another clear vision I have often recollected is of a little old English lady peering out of her flat and into the hall as I was running away. She had a white sleeping cap over a head of curlers, and a pink robe with white stitching. I have asked myself how the heck I remember those details. I wonder what she was thinking as I bolted past her in my underwear.

So I ran and ran and ran through the streets of London, eventually ending up at Hyde Park. I tossed everything under some large bushes, got dressed, and entered the park grounds. I sat on a bench, dazed, for over an hour. I decided I'd sleep there until dawn, at which point I'd catch the Underground to Heathrow and a TWA flight back to the sanctuary of home.

My sleep got interrupted by two bobbies on night patrol; one of them prodded me with his baton and demanded that I grab my things and exit the premises. After I saw the pair walk about two hundred meters around a bend, I reentered and found another bench to lie on.

The bobbies made their second round and, of course, found me stretched out horizontally. They were less polite this time when asking me to leave. I again gathered my belongings, got escorted out of the park, and proceeded to walk aimlessly down the dim streets into the cool night air. The drama of the evening had started to wear on my ability to remain coherent.

I found a bank across the street from an Underground station and decided to rest upright on its steps until tube service began, at which point I could catch the first train to Heathrow. Once again, a bobby approached. As he questioned me, I mumbled in a defeated manner that the past five hours had been difficult.

I wanted him to disappear but he did not. I didn't know if he was suspicious of me or if in fact he had measured the depth of my anxieties and actually wanted to help.

After filling him in on the details of my drama, a story he appeared genuinely affected by, he asked me if I knew the address of Ken the Jamaican's flat. I responded "no" and pleaded that I just wanted to get out of England.

He asked me if I'd be comfortable following him back to his flat, where I could shower (I was covered with mud from getting dressed in the bushes of Hyde Park), and where he would prepare breakfast for me, after which he would give me a lift to the airport. I accepted his offer (people sometimes call me an idiot at this point of the story).

It turned out Andy Andrews the Bobby was a good man wanting to help a scared kid. He later dropped me off at the airport and I caught a flight back to Los Angeles, never telling anyone of this experience until I was into my twenties.

* * *

Karen and I got married on May 19, 1984, in Phoenix, Arizona. On the morning of our wedding, a family member informed me that "someone named Andy" had just arrived from London for the nuptials. "Who?" I asked. Andy and I had only communicated four times in seven years, through letters. Because I had always appreciated what he had done for me that crazy evening in London, I had sent him our wedding announcement as a courtesy. He obviously hadn't understood it was not an actual invitation.

For the first time in his life, Andy the Bobby had left the UK for another country, showing up in Arizona without telling me a thing. Surprisingly, he had made lodging reservations for the first night only, and he otherwise seemed completely lost in his foreign environment. My parents graciously offered him their home in Southern California for the entirety of his two-week stay. Mom and Dad told me Andy was so intrigued by the vastness of the open land between Phoenix and Southern California that he stared out the window for the four hundred-mile drive home, in awe. He spent his time in America in a gardening euphoria, amazed at how well the plants grew in my parents' sun-drenched yard.

*   *   *

During our first-anniversary vacation, in London, Karen and I visited Andy's flat. We stayed in touch with him until he stopped responding to our communications in the late '80s. I believe he passed away during that time, which saddens me for many reasons. First, Andy was a decent man. But he also struggled through a life of challenges related to his own progressive disease: He battled debilitating diabetes. On the morning he helped me in 1977, as he made me breakfast, he described how his eyes were failing him (he was nearly legally blind), how he was now single (he insinuated his wife had left him after years of marriage), and that he would soon he forced out of the police ranks due to his illness. At the time, I was a teenager who had very little empathy for such worries—his issues weren't relatable to me. In retrospect, he appeared somber and I wish I would have expressed more concern for his circumstances. Andy was one of those unfortunate people traveling the road of chronic illness mostly alone.

The Englishman gave us a nice bottle of 1963 port as a wedding gift in 1984. One day in 2007, Karen asked me if we were ever going to drink "Andy's port." I was amazed we still had the special wine, and later asked a Portland *sommelier* what we should expect when drinking the now forty-five-year-old port, as we hadn't properly cared for the bottle since our wedding day. She told us we should drink it soon and expect something unbearable or something magical.

Andy's wedding-gift port was magical! Wow...a truly unique taste and special memory. We shared it with decades-long friends Dan the Man and Parmie, celebrating both of our wedding anniversaries.

Cheers to you, Andy.

CHAPTER 15

Harvard in the Desert

Through all the absurdity, I somehow grew up.

P AUL, A PAL since grade school, once commented, "Kenny, you went to Arizona State one person and came back another." He was right. It was liberating to experience life beyond the town and life I had known for eighteen years. To begin anew. To spread my wings.

University life is a special opportunity to redefine parts of who we are, or who we want to become. Most young people stepping onto campus evolve by growing in confidence, ambition, and focus. My father had told me from an early age I would love the college experience; he was spot on with his proclamation.

I followed Good Buddy Ron to Arizona State University with a short-term plan of living at his townhouse in Scottsdale. Because I needed a longer-term housing solution and wanted to live closer to campus, I decided to rush the fraternities. The first house Ron and I visited was Sigma Nu, which we both pledged and lived at during uniquely transformational years.

There were 38,000 undergraduate students attending Arizona State when I arrived in 1979, making it one of the largest educational institutions in the country. *U.S. News & World Report* listed the school among the top five academic institutions in the United States that year, along with Harvard, Stanford, Princeton, and Duke. (The veracity of this statement remains unsubstantiated.) While the campus was sprawling, the areas surrounding it offered a smaller-town look and feel.

The Devils House dance club pumped out great rock 'n' roll music or tracks from Michael Jackson's megahit album, *Thriller.* Some of the restaurants holding special memories for Karen, my buddies, and me still exist: the Chuckbox, Bandersnatch, and Minder Binders (a favored hangout and the home of Burger Madness on Thursday nights). Today, ASU's expanded complex of upscale dining and lodging encircling the campus has, in my opinion, stolen some of its earlier college-town charm.

Living in the Sigma Nu compound was nonstop entertainment. Sixty young men with diverse backgrounds, personalities, and interests exploring total independence together. Parties, sororities, athletics, beer, and chaos. It was all so wonderful that it felt like a dream.

The Greek-life experience positively affected my personal growth. Unfortunately, in today's reality, where shenanigans seem to have evolved into sexual assault, hazing deaths, and felonious activities, I believe most fraternities are better avoided than joined. But I got lucky: Sigma Nu at ASU in 1979 was managed by a group of sharp upperclassmen committed to not becoming the generalized *Animal House* of John Belushi fame.

The house leadership tilted toward Midwesterners and I remain impressed with many of these (now middle-aged) men. Running for office was always encouraged, and winning an election typically required actual effort to be successful. That said, my stint as vice president, or what was officially termed lieutenant commander, was, much like our federal government's equivalent, a position of relatively few meaningful contributions.

Blind Luck

Our life journeys typically, eventually, lead us down the best paths. As fate would have it, the woman I was meant to spend my future with was literally right across the street from my fraternity, in Manzanita Hall, the same towering triangular dorm building, with those huge windows begging "aim here," that we would drive golf balls into from our house two hundred yards away.

Sigma Nu had a Little Sister social program for young women who had chosen to participate in the Greek system without joining sororities. The program matched each prospective Little Sister with a Sigma Nu Big Brother, and it was the Little Sisters who selected the men to be paired with.

My future wife asked for advice from one of the current Little Sisters regarding who might be worthwhile to select as her Big Brother. Her friend (thank you, Paige!) put a star next to the names of ten or fifteen men, and because Cruickshank began with a C, I was now the first person alphabetically on Karen's list, thus she selected me.

Each Big Brother was then asked to take his new Little Sister out for a drink or meal to get acquainted. Because I had a girlfriend at the time, I was often busy, and I had missed the meet-and-greet where everyone got introduced. I had no idea who Karen Busch was or what she looked like. Fortunately, my new Sigma Nu buddy, Dan the Man, remembered her quite clearly.

On the day of my first encounter with Karen, as Dan the Man and I waited for her while seated on a brick wall outside Manzanita Hall, he pointed toward this beautiful, tall, bronzed, and beaming young woman exiting the dormitory, and whispered, "That's her."

My first words were, "Wow, she's pretty."

Karen became a good friend. In fact, months after our introduction, Dan and I would sometimes pick up a large Domino's pizza and a six-pack of beer and head to her new apartment, where I'd tell her about my dating and personal life. She was patient, smart, and artistic, and our friendship grew over the ensuing one and a half years.

The following summer I sent her a postcard from Europe with the words "Will you marry me?" scribbled on the back. I intended it to be a bit of humor, though there was obviously a budding affection for this amazing woman. Six months after sending her that postcard, I asked her out on our first date. It was a memorable one.

My Urban Assault Vehicle Fiat (I could write a book about the car's exploits, which included getting wedged between two poles meant to keep cars from driving onto the campus walkways) had been so badly thrashed by fraternity brothers and rugby teammates that I asked Good Buddy Ron if I could borrow his much nicer GMC Jimmy truck for the important first dinner with Karen. He was happy to oblige, and he commented it was about time I had asked her out. I picked her up and we drove to a nice (but affordable!) restaurant in Scottsdale for the first serious test of a possible future together. At least, that was my objective.

Ron failed to inform me he had just installed expensive off-road lights on top of his huge vehicle (this is called "assigning blame"). It was dark when I first entered the truck so I hadn't noticed the new accessories. When the restaurant's underground parking structure cautioned of a seven-foot clearance maximum, I brushed the warning off, knowing the vehicle I was driving was only a few inches taller than me.

As I drove under the first cement crossbeam, Ron's brand new expensive off-road spotlights were compressed into the roof of the truck cabin, just above our heads. There was a cacophony of crunching metal sounds. I was surprised and Karen appeared shocked, but upon quick reflection, realizing there was no solution to the problem, I told her, "Well, the damage is done. Let's park and eat." As we drove below several more cement beams to reach our parking spot, there was further ear-piercing scraping at every passing.

The truck's damage notwithstanding, my first date with Karen was a resounding success. Halfway through our meal, I told myself I was going to marry this woman.

The Marine Corps

Because I had always assumed I would become a military and commercial pilot, in 1980 I decided to take a big step toward that goal by applying for Platoon Leaders Class (PLC), Officer Candidate School (OCS), United States Marine Corps. The program was split into junior- and senior-year college sessions held in Quantico, Virginia.

To qualify, I needed to perform at a certain level on an officer-candidate exam. My frat brothers had learned I was to take the test on a Saturday. That morning, I walked outside to my Urban Assault Vehicle Fiat and found it perched on blocks and absent its four wheels. I called the USMC test center to let them know I wouldn't be able to make it that day. They informed me it was not unusual for young men to keep their buddies from taking the exam, thereby steering their comrades away from dangerous military assignments.

I understood that the fact my wheels were missing (and later found dangling from a flagpole two miles away) had nothing to do with such noble intentions. I knew it had everything to do with a late night, cheap beer (or perhaps Thunderbird and Mad Dog 2020), and boredom.

Before I left for what I good-naturedly termed "my jarhead

adventure," my father provided me with excellent counsel. He said, "They will try to break you down with mental games and physical challenges. Approach it with a sense of humor. Understand their goals are to push people to their limits and to see who cracks." He was right.

When we arrived on base in Quantico, I had wavy light hair, was wearing a necklace, and lived in California—three big strikes against me. As I stepped off the bus, the drill sergeant yelled at me to get in line, and then he barked, "What's your name, Candidate?"

I replied, "Ken Cruickshank."

Colossal mistake. He got in my face and, with his saliva flicking onto my cheeks and nose, he screamed, "What the [bleep] did you say? You stupid [bleep]. You stupid [bleep] with a stupid [slur] necklace. Where the [bleep] are you from?"

"California."

He responded, "You ask for permission to speak, you stupid [bleep] candidate. You say, 'Candidate Cruickshank requests permission to speak.'"

I responded, "OK."

"Goddammit, Cruickshank, you are one dumb [bleep] necklace-wearing [slur] from California. You ask for permission to speak *every time* you open your goddam mouth. Candidate Cruickshank, I want you to remove your [slur] necklace."

I removed my necklace, then he screamed, "Candidate Cruickshank, why are you here?"

I began to do exactly as my father had suggested. I had taken this initial screening experience with a grain of salt and a sense of humor. As several drill instructors were yelling at other PLC OCS candidates—great young men I was privileged to have met—I thought I could pick up the nuances of "the game" based on the questions and answers being shouted out.

So, when asked why I was standing in Quantico, Virginia,

on this (darn) hot summer day, I responded, "Candidate Cruickshank requests permission to speak!"

"Permission granted."

"Candidate Cruickshank wants to become a United States Marine Corps pilot!"

His final response was classic: "That's a great goal, Candidate Cruickshank, but you might be too [bleep] stupid to make it happen."

The next morning, I awoke from a deep slumber inside a Quonset hut through the sounds of a metal trash can being flung against the wall—it was still dark outside. So started my PLC OCS training; it became one of the highlight experiences of my young life.

The mess hall walls displayed photos and captions of young officers who had made the ultimate sacrifices for their fellow soldiers and country. I grew unsettled by how many of the men had lost their lives jumping on live grenades. I remember processing all the ways I could protect a platoon without actually pouncing on a small bomb.

My father was right about the inevitable fallout; several men could not handle the physical and mental extremes we experienced, and they would disappear from the barracks one day, never to return. After I had graduated from the first of two summer stints comprising the program, I was certain I would return the following summer to complete the training, after which I would graduate from Arizona State before traveling to Pensacola, Florida, for ten more weeks of officer training, then flight school.

I had performed well during the seven weeks and I was deeply proud of what I had accomplished, perhaps prouder than at any point in my life. At graduation, as Captain Lilley thanked me for my hard work, and as he mentioned he was looking forward to my participation in the final program the following summer,

I looked him squarely in the eyes while shaking his hand and said, "I will definitely be back, sir."

I never returned. There were a few key reasons why I ultimately decided against a career as a Marine officer. The first was that as I got to know many of the candidates personally, understanding their intentions for entering the military, I began to feel guilty about the reasons I was there, and the plan I held. While I was then, and am still today, a patriotic American who feels blessed to have grown up in this country, I had no intention of staying in the Corps beyond the six-year commitment required after acceptance into their pilot program. My goal was to earn my flight time, travel, wear cool uniforms, complete my obligation, and begin a career as a commercial airline pilot—just as Dad had.

The young men I had met through OCS affected that plan. I was in awe of these future heroes. Many were not short-termers interested in bailing after a six-year commitment; rather, they sought ten-, twenty-, and thirty-year careers in the Marines. It was humbling.

Another reason I never returned to Quantico resulted from a conversation I had with a group of Navy and Marine pilots at a bar in Washington, DC, while on weekend leave. They looked like they were in their late twenties. Their uniforms dazzled me, as did their tales of flying F-15s and F-18s. The topic turned to women, and they asked me if I was in a serious relationship. Before I could answer, one of them blurted out, "You'll never be home; don't get serious."

The comment stuck with me. My father was often gone during my childhood. His absence was even more glaring to my older brothers and sisters and, of course, to my mother. The issue of leaving a wife and children at home too often resonated with me, and it eventually evolved into being a major factor influencing my decision to exit PLC OCS in 1982.

Ironically, as a businessman in a Fortune 50 firm, I probably spent as much time (or more) on airplanes and away from home than professional pilots do. In today's global business environment, balancing travel time with family time is a common challenge.

Six months before graduation from ASU, I told the Marines I was pulling out of the OCS program. I didn't give them my reasons, which included my budding interest in a coed. Her name was Karen.

*   *   *

I loved my father, Captain Dick, for many reasons, including some of the sincere advice he delivered. His reaction to my decision not to pursue a career as a pilot in the Marine Corps and the commercial airlines surprised me. I thought he would be deeply disappointed, perhaps even slightly angered, by my decision not to attend the second summer of OCS.

Instead, Dad's reaction (and Mom's) was supportive. He said he understood the reasons for my decision and respected them. Then he advised me to change my major to something else I might be good at. He suggested I had the skills and acumen required in the corporate world and recommended I pursue a business degree. After a period of considering my options, I changed my major from Air Transportation to General Business.

Isn't it interesting how, despite even long-held ambitions, our life journeys can change unexpectedly, pushing us in new directions we later consider fortuitous? I continued to experience worsening symptoms related to my MS just around the time of that conversation about my future, though they were fleeting impairments that, by themselves, would not have affected my career decisions.

But had I pursued my passion of flying in the military, the

USMC would have yanked me out of the cockpit within a few years. Some of my disease symptoms would have automatically disqualified me from the program. Any recognition of my numbness, slowed reflexes, or optic neuritis, as slight as they were, would have meant the end of the government's investment in my flight training.

While multiple sclerosis eventually forced me to stop working at Intel, my high-tech sales and marketing career fulfilled me. Thanks, Dad.

*　*　*

Looking back, I can recognize the second clear manifestation of my multiple sclerosis (though I wouldn't be diagnosed for another decade). I had trained hard prior to my arrival in Quantico and achieved high scores on the battery of physical fitness tests relative to the six hundred men in K Company, with one exception: the three-and-a-half-mile run. I committed myself to regular training in hopes of achieving a faster time.

For the life of me, despite Herculean efforts, I was still mired in the middle of the pack weeks later. After one of the timed trials, other candidates mentioned I appeared to be walking like a horse, flipping my legs out in front of my body and slapping my "hooves" onto the ground. I remember feeling as if I had less control over not just my legs, but my entire body.

I justified the sensations by telling myself I had just run a long distance on a very hot and humid day. However, months later, a young woman made a similar comment about my odd walking manner, just after I had completed a sprint race. Three years later still, my wife's uncle, an orthopedic surgeon, commented to Karen about possibly having observed "an MS gait" after he and I had run together along the shores of Lake Geneva, in Wisconsin. The symptom would ultimately become glaring.

* * *

Dan the Man pledged Sigma Nu a year after I had arrived at ASU. The first time I met him, he had obviously imbibed in a few too many barley pops, and he thus bumped into me rather aggressively as I walked by. He later grew convinced I disliked him and that I'd have him depledged (kicked out), ending his fraternity experience. Instead, Dan and I became extremely close friends. In fact, it was his marriage to Parmie that introduced Karen and me to the beautiful state of Oregon, where we eventually moved to and reside in today.

Dan is frighteningly similar to me in some ways. His sense of humor is almost exactly like mine. We have always been able to finish each other's jokes and stories as if they were our own. We engaged in similar manners of mayhem throughout our time at ASU. I would say he was my best bud in college; the only other candidate for such a distinction, Good Buddy Ron, took his house presidency and responsibilities a bit too seriously for my liking, refusing to get involved in the misconduct necessary to earn such a distinction.

Dan the Man and I share something much more significant than a sense of humor today: We are both afflicted with chronic progressive diseases. While I have had symptoms related to my MS for forty years, he was diagnosed with a spinocerebellar ataxia several years ago. During the early stages of determining his diagnosis, the doctors seriously considered he might be stricken with multiple sclerosis. The irony that either of us once-upon-a-time hell raisers is now saddled with an encumbering illness is surprising. That we both were struck by aggressive autoimmune diseases boggles my mind.

Coincidentally, we are at very similar stages in the management of our symptoms. We are beyond using canes; Dan presently relies on a walker. I drive wheelchairs and scooters; he's too darn proud and stubborn to try them, just as I once was. He'll come around (I keep telling him middle-aged women dig guys in scooters).

Dan sometimes remarks that my personal health situation is direr than his own. I have no idea if that's true. In the end, it does not matter which of us is at whatever stage of deterioration and labeling. We are two great friends who can provide a level of comfort to each other as we travel down our similar but separate roads.

A salute to you, Dan the Man, for many more years of friendship.

CHAPTER 16

Moving On

"Glory days, Yeah they'll pass you by,
Glory days, In the wink of a young girl's eye."
—Bruce Springsteen

PROGRESSIVE DISEASE WILL always rob the afflicted, and what is stolen may be part of your truest essence—the way you fundamentally perceive yourself, or the way others see you. While whatever you are left with will always be more important than anything taken, that realization may not grow obvious for years.

Take a moment to consider your most passionate interests outside of your family, those hobbies or undertakings that bring you (or brought you) the most happiness. Interests that are at the very core of your being, that define you. During my youth and college, my passion was participating in various sports. I am not a professional athlete, but I cannot imagine any pro enjoying his competitions more than I did.

In 1972, I remember being handed a black nylon jacket with white lettering that read "Tustin Eastern Little League All-Star." Being recognized was not the primary thrill; I just wanted an excuse to continue playing after the regular season had ended.

I'd meet my childhood friend, Paul, at his house during weekends in high school to play ping-pong, paddle tennis, and basketball all day long. Literally. Good Buddy Ron and I would strap on boxing gloves for some pugilism fun, or he'd play catcher and I'd throw him fastballs. I rowed crew during my only year at Orange Coast College and loved it. I would run sprints during the week and on weekends simply because it felt good. And I continued to lift weights religiously.

Sports were bound to my psyche. I loved battling and breaking a sweat. If I wasn't exercising, I was contemplating when and where I could, and with whom. When I graduated from high school, I was five feet ten inches and weighed 175 pounds. Upon college graduation in 1982, I weighed 220 pounds and stood nearly six-two. Being bigger and faster enabled new possibilities.

Rugby, which I played for ASU, was the sport that stirred my soul. I hold many special memories from those days, perhaps exemplified by a four-day stretch with my teammates in 1982. We competed in a tournament in San Diego, while wearing nylon mesh jerseys that our competitors considered sacrilegious (cotton jerseys were too stifling in the Arizona desert heat). Everyone in the rugby world understood that Canterbury long-sleeved jerseys from New Zealand were the *only* appropriate attire for true ruggers. Despite the ridicule, the "guys from Arizona with the lame jerseys" throttled every team we faced, up to the final against OMBAC (Old Mission Bay Athletic Club), a perennial national club champion with older and international players. We lost in a close match, our heads held high.

After the games, we drove to my parents' home in Orange County for dinner and sleep. I was silently concerned about our arrival because, well, these were rugby players, and rugby players generally hold (well-deserved) reputations for rowdiness. My teammates entered the house appearing fierce, with dried sweat, bloodstains, and bruises, but they behaved as perfect gentlemen while eating from my mother's finest china. It is still a special memory for Mom.

The following morning, we drove to Los Angeles for a match against UCLA. We dominated play except in one key category: scoring. That single blemish to our conference record prevented us from moving on to the West Coast collegiate regionals as the Southwestern representative.

Random glimpses of my diseased future continued to appear. During my senior year at ASU, I played in a softball tournament and our team made it to the championship game. With two outs and a man on second base in the bottom of the final inning, the batter drilled a line drive straight at me. I literally did not have to move my feet to catch the ball. I held out my leather, the ball entered the webbing, and we won the tournament. At least, that's what I thought had just happened. But actually, the ball had gone straight through my glove and kept rolling to the outfield fence. By the time I realized I had not trapped the ball, both runners were well on their way toward scoring, and we lost the game.

That darn left hand of mine—the one fitted with the mitt— had already begun to lose some of its strength and dexterity at age twenty-two. A few years later, balls were popping out of my glove far too often, so I stopped playing softball. A year after that, I played in my last rugby match. Soon, playing any sport competitively was a pipe dream.

As an athlete, I peaked at age twenty-one. I never ran faster or jumped further than I did at that age. I never played rugby, or any other sport, as well as I did in 1981, despite continuing a comprehensive workout regimen.

While the college experience can redefine parts of who we are or who we want to be, some things never change. Sports were always a constant for me, and I had assumed I would be wringing the sweat out of my headband into my sixties. Multiple sclerosis peeled away layers of my identity when it diminished my ability to engage in something I loved doing. Ultimately, I transitioned, finding joy in new pursuits. It was a slow process. Yet today, in the deepest recesses of my mind, I still identify as an athlete.

I believe in heaven. I trust that one day I will again be able to run down a pitch with reckless abandon. I envision passing a rugby ball to my son (a hundred years from now), sharing the thrills of competition on a sunny day and a thick green field. It is a treasured anticipation.

* * *

The Resilience of Repute

In 1984, during our engagement, I drove from Orange County to Phoenix to visit Karen's family, and to help with some wedding preparations. I had brought my mail from home and left it on the counter of her parents' kitchen. While I was occupied, my future mother-in-law flipped through a current issue of a Sigma Nu newsletter I had left atop the pile.

Inside the publication was a section titled "Remember When." The first story written described how, in 1981, a naked Ken Cruickshank had jumped into an unmanned police car and driven it away. The article needed editing: I was not naked.

What really transpired that night was that, after our entire house had streaked *au naturel* across campus and around the sororities, some brothers were confronted by the campus police, who were always easy to flee from, but also by a Tempe police officer. He (nonsensically) stopped his car in the middle of the road and began chasing the last small band of frolicking naked men down fraternity row. Smartly, after the trailing party of criminals realized that returning to their own frat would implicate not only them but the rest of us, they scurried down the street and dispersed among the other Greek houses.

I was standing on the balcony at the top of our frat house stairs and decided it would be darn funny to hide the unoccupied police car behind the ASU baseball complex, which stood about a quarter-mile away. So I ran to the vehicle (again, fully clothed, for the record), jumped inside, and began to drive away. *Victory!*

Not quite. I observed another police car speeding up the road directly toward me. I determined I had better devise a plausible explanation for commandeering a Tempe police car. I pulled over sharply to the curb, turned the ignition off, and sprang from the driver's seat. This is what happened next, and I am telling it as true as a compass (there's a Tempe police officer—somewhere—and a whole bunch of Sigma Nus who can validate this story).

After hopping out, I stepped toward the approaching cop's door as his vehicle screeched to a halt at my feet, and when he threw his door open I quickly explained that the previous officer had left his car blocking traffic, and I had only moved it to "free up road congestion." Then I pointed down fraternity row and exclaimed, "He went that way," just like they do in the movies. And yes, remarkably, he jumped back inside, slammed his door, pressed the gas pedal, and sped down the street—just like in the movies.

Of course, I realize absconding with a police cruiser was one of the dumbest things I've ever attempted. No student would get away with such foolishness today. *But it just had to be done.*

My future mother-in-law was so disturbed reading the account of my actions that she sought advice from her college-age son, John, about what to do with this information. Until then, she'd held a fairly positive opinion of her future son-in-law, but she had suddenly grown unsettled through her recent field intelligence. Her reaction again reminded me that few mothers could have handled the crazy antics associated with raising the ten Cruickshank children, where such adventures were not unusual. John counseled his mother to relax, that it was likely an exaggerated event (it was; I was not naked), and that this news was not the tip of an iceberg of deviant behavior.

He was mostly correct.

PART III

Ours Is a Family Journey

Illness breaks us down;
family rebuilds and sustains us.

CHAPTER 17

Love and Life for My Son

Cats have nine lives. Sons do not.
There were times when I worried. Worried a lot.

Ken, b. 1987

MY SON KEN and I have a wonderful relationship today, and I am so proud of the person he is that I sometimes ask myself if I really deserve to have this special young man as my child. Particularly considering some difficult moments he experienced that I profoundly regret.

There was a period of my employment when I literally worked every day, weekend, and holiday for three straight years (and I don't mean just reading emails). I am not proud of this; I was a young and immature manager trying to rise through the ranks at Intel, and for too long I was also incapable of pushing back on management's requests. It was not a company problem; it was mine. I sometimes overburdened the members of my team by proposing or accepting projects that resulted in insane workloads. I inevitably put myself in positions of having to work day and night to help deliver the results expected or promised. I was pushing myself as hard as I possibly could, fatiguing and stressing my body. At the same time, my MS had begun to increasingly affect my mental and physical health.

This doesn't mean some of the stupid things I said or did should be excused; it only suggests I was unwilling to make the necessary adjustments to my lifestyle, changes that would have significantly reduced my stress levels and preserved diminishing energy. But it was my way to just barrel ahead, using the demands of my job as an excuse for a life occasionally out of balance, or for poor decisions I made.

Valentine's Day Massacre

I had come home late from the office one evening and the family had already eaten dinner. Because I had been regularly missing meals, Karen set an ultimatum for me: "The kids and I will be eating at 6:30 each evening; we'd love for you to join us."

For months, possibly even years, she'd call me at my desk and ask that I make it home to eat by a specific time. When I wouldn't show up, she would call me to get an adjusted ETA, and I would apologize and tell her I'd be home in thirty minutes. Sometimes, I still wouldn't make it in time to join the family.

After arriving home too late one evening, I noticed Kenny had spread Valentine cards across the kitchen table. His teacher had requested that he fill out a card for every student in class, something he didn't want to do. Earlier, Kenny and Karen had debated the issue and she'd finally told him he could discuss it with his father. I was blunt and told him I wanted him to fill out a card for every classmate, *right now*, end of discussion. I assumed that was exactly what he would do. The next morning, I left for some meetings in Los Angeles.

After a long day with customers, I drove south to my parents' place in Orange County. I was a bit on edge because of a grueling schedule, but it was still nice to see my folks while enjoying a home-cooked meal. Then the phone rang and my mother handed me the receiver.

Karen informed me Kenny had been called into the principal's office because he had added the word "don't" to his female classmates' Valentine cards, so they now read "I *don't* like you," except for one young lady's card (he had considered her special). Moreover, he had signed one of the boys' cards with the word "Asshole," a term that had become all the rage among his peers after it had been presented to them by one of their high school-aged brothers. None of the justifications mattered; I was livid and demanded that Karen put Kenny on the phone. She measured my tone and advised me to be calm.

I was not calm. Instead, when Kenny got on the line I screamed at him, asking how he could disappoint me so much. I kept him on the phone for five minutes, chastising him more than any father ever should for such a juvenile protest. I still consider it pitiful that I had such a damning reaction.

After delivering my judgment, I hung up the phone and walked down the hall to my parents' guest room. Mom and Dad followed me and hovered around, eventually telling me they had been meaning to talk to me about something "for some time." They proceeded to explain I was being too tough on Kenny, that I needed to lighten up, that he was only a young child, and that he shouldn't be scolded as he just had been.

I calmly informed them it was none of their business and I would handle things the way I saw fit. They walked away silently. After fifteen minutes of contemplation, I remember staring at my reflection in a dresser mirror and growing appalled with myself. I was hit by a freight train of regret and enlightenment.

My relationship with my son was literally changed forever that night. Some readers will assume I am exaggerating. I am not.

I got back on the phone with Karen and asked to speak with

Kenny. She told me that whatever I had said earlier seemed to have overwhelmed him. That poor boy, my dear son—I had torn his heart out. Karen went to find him, knowing, through the tone of my voice, that I needed to reconcile, to apologize. Again, she advised gentleness.

After speaking with Kenny, it was clear he had been so affected by my words that he was unable to fully process the anger I had exhibited. How unfortunate is it that a father would be infuriated by his ten-year-old son writing "I don't like you" or even "Asshole" on a bunch of third-grade Valentine cards?

The moral for me was to constantly express my unconditional love and support to our children, and to dole out any disciplinary words and actions appropriately. It was not enough to be a good father ninety-five percent of the time, if the other five percent might be my crushing disapproval. I am thankful for my parents' intervention, and for me being able to grasp the significance of the moment. Clearly, my education wasn't complete, but these lessons accumulated and, eventually, helped me do the right things.

Karen was not just a fly on the wall during this phase; she was and is the key influence within our family. I am sure she had let it be known I was being overly harsh on Kenny, in her temperate and typically effective manner. But I believe that at that specific point in my life, regarding the issue of my disciplining of Kenny, being confronted by my parents' words and disappointed expressions forced me to face an uncomfortable truth.

Can a single event profoundly change who we are or who we want to be? I believe the answer is an unmitigated *yes*. I have fervently apologized to Ken for my reaction that evening years ago, but he insists it was no big deal, even that he doesn't remember it very well. He likely remembers it quite well; he's just a forgiving son. He's also patient, compassionate, and devoted. He'll be a good father.

We often evolve from within, but sometimes it's the people who care about us most who lead the way to epiphanies and personal growth. We just need to listen.

Precious Life

We could have lost Ken in an accident at age sixteen, and again at twenty-five. During finals week in high school, we let him drive to school; he had exhibited a healthy level of caution the previous months of driving with Karen or me in the car. We had waited months to cut him loose, as we live in the hills of Portland where the roads are twisting with narrow shoulders and steep drop-offs. But he had earned our confidence and we were unconcerned on the morning he left for his exams. It was a dry and beautiful day.

Just as Karen was about to leave the house with Caitlin and Bre, fulfilling her role in the daily carpooling duty, Ken called the house to explain to Karen he had "driven off the road" in route to school. Karen asked, "Into a ditch?" He replied, "Kind of." He was calm as he spoke, requesting that she or Dad drive to meet him—he was less than two miles away.

Unbeknownst to us, he was being coached to remain composed as he was speaking to his mother.

Fatigued by disease, I typically began my day later than Karen and the kids due to long hours of sleep, but having overheard Karen's conversation, it made sense for me to roll out of bed and to drive to Ken. I hopped into my old BMW dressed in sweats, threw my cane onto the passenger seat, and headed down Skyline Road.

My heart rate soared as I viewed two fire trucks, two police cars, and an ambulance blocking the street. I rolled down my window to speak with a police officer but he interrupted and told me to turn around. Instead I drove past him and parked in between the trucks and the roadside. I peered down the hill and was horrified by the image of my SUV lying upside down fifty feet below. I grabbed my cane and moved toward the road shoulder, confronted by the officer I'd driven past.

Several firemen and a police officer were surrounding the damaged SUV. The only thing I could muster to scream was, "Where's my son?" The emergency workers halted and stared up the hill at me. One of them responded, "Your son is okay; he's at the house next door speaking with the police."

Ken explained to me he had tried to avoid a dog in the road and had inadvertently gotten the two right-side tires off the pavement, next to the steep decline. He instinctively turned the wheel to the left, assuming the SUV would pop back onto the pavement, but instead it fell backward before rolling and flipping end-over-end, ultimately resting upside down on a gravel driveway cut from the hillside. Had that gravel drive not halted the tumbling vehicle, he would have rolled another one hundred steep feet into timber.

Ken told us later that, as the car fell backward, his last thought was of being badly hurt (I shudder at that recollection of his fear). One of the policemen told me he had seen people killed in lesser accidents, and that having his seatbelt buckled may have saved Ken's life.

After dealing with the authorities and measuring Ken's physical well-being, I asked him if he was mentally okay for school and his finals, and he told me he was. *What was I thinking?* I should have just taken him home for the day. He bombed his final and didn't tell anyone at school about the accident. The parent who had picked him up told me Ken had acted normally on the drive home, that he had never mentioned anything about the incident.

That's because our son was in shock. Later in the day, we noticed he couldn't hold his drink steady in his hand. That afternoon, Ken decided to take a nap upstairs. Thirty minutes later, Caitlin came down from her bedroom to tell Karen that her brother was yelling for her. When Karen opened his bedroom door, he was asleep but restless in his bed, apparently reliving the day's drama and calling out to his mother. Karen's eyes moistened.

She was overwhelmed with emotion the next morning, when she strode into the kitchen and found Ken sitting at the table eating a bowl of cereal. A simple, cherished moment.

*   *   *

The final act of this story is interesting. I am typically annoyed by people claiming to see the face of Jesus on a grilled cheese sandwich, or the image of Mary on a tortilla. Such stories seem irreverent to me. I listen to or read accounts of divine interventions with what I feel are healthy levels of skepticism.

That said, the following details display a mysterious moment in our family's lives worthy of deeper reflection. I have learned in my lifetime to accept that some truths are much stranger than fiction.

Weeks before Ken's accident, in her home in New Jersey, my sister Fran and her three children held hands and prayed for Ken's safety as a new driver. Her daughter Madison cut out and painted an angel. The picture had the words "Guardian Angel" penned across it, and on the backside was a prayer for Ken's safety.

One day while I was driving with Ken, a week before his accident, I found the cutout angel on the floor of the front passenger compartment. I studied it and asked him where he had gotten it. He replied that Aunt Fran and his cousins had sent it to him. I told him I thought that was a wonderful gesture and said he should keep it in the car. I placed it in the glove box, then I forgot about it.

On the day of the accident, after I had called Karen on her cell phone to let her know the severity of Ken's accident, she rushed to the scene with her carpool of kids, who still needed to get to school. As she neared the area, one of the boys looked down the hill and exclaimed, "Mrs. Cruickshank, the car's down there!" Her heart sank and panic burst forth.

After Karen had approached and embraced Ken, and shed tears of thanks for his safety, Caitlin left her side and walked over to the totaled vehicle to grab some of Ken's belongings, accompanied by a police officer. The front windshield had been shattered and was lying on the grass next to the upside-down vehicle.

Caitlin had never seen the painted angel with the prayer, but on the evening of the accident she informed us she had seen an angel image within the shattered windshield, telling us it was beautiful, that "the angel looked like it was embedded in ice." I told our sweet fourteen-year-old that that was impossible, because the angel was in the glove box.

I drove to the wrecking yard the following day and found the cut-out in the glove box, as expected. Regardless, Caitlin insists to this day she saw a beautiful angel lying within the shattered, ice-like windshield.

Why shouldn't I believe that, too? The wonder of some things cannot be explained away.

*　*　*

In 2013, my sister Fran's husband, Wayne, was in a terrible accident in Northern California. The convertible sports car he was driving, with his stepfather as passenger, inexplicably accelerated, lost its rear suspension stability, and crashed into a single-story home in a neighborhood. Wayne's stepfather was thrown from the car (he fully recovered).

Unfortunately, Wayne got knocked unconscious during the

accident. After impact with the house, the fuel tank began to leak and caught fire; the vehicle and the home burst into flames. The Good Samaritans on the scene could not pull Wayne from the wreckage due to the intense heat. Strangers sprayed water on him and screamed for him to "move to the right!"

He eventually regained consciousness and made his way to the opposite side of the car, where he dropped himself to the ground and was pulled to safety. He received severe burns over twenty percent of his body, including along the left side of his face, neck, scalp, shoulder, arm, and back. He was in the burn unit for almost two months, having to overcome intense pain and multiple grafting surgeries. He continues to heal, though the trauma left him without his left ear and with some scarring. My sister and their children are, of course, singularly thankful he's home, and alive.

Fran sat by Wayne's side in the burn unit as often as was allowed during his surgeries and recovery. Soon thereafter, I reminded her of the Guardian Angel and prayer she and their children had prayed over and sent to Ken just before his accident. Is it possible that her loving actions were rewarded by an angel waking Wayne from his unconsciousness and helping him to move from the flames of the sports car? She believes it is all somehow connected.

Talk of angels is typically scoffed at today. Religious texts include essential accounts regarding angels, written by and for Jews, Christians, and Muslims. I have read that every person is assigned a Guardian Angel to guide and protect. I do not believe this means all of us will be kept out of harm's way, rather that we will never be alone in this world or during transition to the next. If I can accept that our universe is comprised of one hundred billion trillion stars, as many astronomers and astrophysicists believe, but that we inhabit the lone sphere supporting human life, then I only need a touch of imagination to embrace Guardian Angels as real. We all believe in something.

Changing Course

Ken graduated from the University of Oregon with an economics degree in 2009. He began his career as a financial advisor, a job he enjoyed and learned a great deal from. Karen and I fully supported his career choice and were relieved he had gained employment in a difficult post-financial-crash economy. We were also selfishly thankful he would be living and working in Oregon.

Two terrible experiences changed his life journey.

One evening in 2011, he walked downstairs (he was still living with us at the time) looking great with a big smile on his face. His financial advising business was growing, he had a new watch on his left wrist, and he was wearing a custom-tailored sport coat for the very first time. I smiled as he left the house, pleased that he would be spending social time with his buddies in downtown Portland.

Later in the evening, after Ken had left his friends at the bar and walked toward his parked car, he got attacked from behind and had no chance to fully defend himself. I will never forget the look in Ken's eyes as he later described the experience to me. I felt sick.

Silently, I wanted to track the offenders down and harm them. My brothers called to say they were willing to fly to Portland to deliver vigilante justice. I understood all our reactions were prompted by the pain of a loved one being senselessly attacked, but our thoughts of retribution were emotionally charged nonsense. It happened, it was disturbing, but it was also time for Ken to begin to heal and to move beyond the mental burden.

We assumed Ken's misfortunes were now a thing of the

past, that rolling off the hillside in our SUV and getting beaten downtown were the last harrowing episodes of his young life. We were wrong.

In 2012, after the Oregon Ducks had defeated Washington in a football game in Eugene, Oregon, Ken was walking through a treed area near Autzen Stadium to meet his friends in a parking lot. A group of male students from the University of Washington noticed him climbing over a wrought iron fence wearing his Oregon colors, and they called out mockingly, as young men are sometimes prone to do. Ken reminded them of the score of the game, an Oregon blowout, after which one of the men in the group ran toward him as he was perched unsteadily on top of the fence. The man grabbed and rattled the fence rods, and Ken fell backward.

I am assuming the assailant thought Ken was dirtied but otherwise okay as he and his group of Washington Huskies departed. If the young man had realized what he had just done, I'm sure he would have stopped to help our son.

At the base of the metal fence, one of the shorter decorative posts was bent outward at the base. The stake was pointing upwards, with an arrow-shaped end and a very small ball at the tip of the arrowhead. Ken fell sideways onto the metal rod and was impaled, the shaft pushing four and a half inches into the side of his chest.

Ken was now alone in a lightly trafficked area off the beaten path, and he was bleeding profusely. He was precariously positioned and slowly realized the gravity of his predicament. He was stunned, in shock, and understood that if he were not discovered, or could not free himself, he could die. Because the spike was pressing against his lung, he was unable to call out for help.

I cringe every time I recall him describing the sucking sound of the post being pulled back out of his body as he used all his strength to push away, freeing himself. I am pausing as I write this; it's difficult to consider how dire the situation was, that he could have succumbed.

Karen and I were at the coast when I received a text message Ken had sent from an emergency room in Portland that some friends had delivered him to. He explained he was being transferred by ambulance from St. Vincent's Hospital to Oregon Health and Science University's trauma unit. He advised us everything was fine and that he'd update us when he knew more. Obviously, our instincts told us to drive to OHSU immediately.

Walking into the trauma unit hospital room, seeing our son laid out with a big patch over his chest, was heart-wrenching. He was clearly in great pain, even though he tried to assuage our concerns. Doctors confirmed his lungs were okay. The rod had missed his heart and a vital artery.

It wasn't long after this incident that Ken decided to move to Orange County to begin a new career. It is my opinion that the beating and impaling experiences were significant facilitators for his choice to head south. He had already decided to change industries; he would now be moving from his hometown to forge a new life. We understood.

Ken is now in the M&A business in Newport Beach, working for Harvey & Company LLC. He's trying to get used to the high rent he's paying for his one-bedroom apartment close to his office. But he loves his job, loves Orange County, and loves his life.

Ken coordinated a wonderful thirtieth anniversary surprise for Karen and me, attended by family and friends at one of our favorite restaurants in downtown Portland, in 2014. He gave us a touching toast and speech that evening. I was so proud of him. Two months later, he gave a beautiful eulogy at my father-in-law's funeral in Lake Geneva, Wisconsin. Again, I grew impressed.

Two years ago, after having read Ken's account of the aftermath of one of my falls in our home, a narrative that opens this memoir, I realized my deteriorating health and subsequent accidents had been much more difficult for him to deal with than I had understood at the time. It is another lesson learned through my life and MS journey: Our sons are not immune to any of the emotional trials within our families. It is a foolish, outdated perspective for fathers to believe otherwise, a flawed paradigm many men of past generations grew up with.

I am like most fathers; I love my son very much. I have tried to impart to him as much wisdom as possible. Every dad has something relevant and important to pass on. What Ken doesn't realize is that when I study his life, I find I have been bettered as a father and mentor because of his example. I have learned much from him.

CHAPTER 18

A Ray of Sunshine

The glass is never half empty.

Caitlin, b. 1989

OUR CHILDREN ARE special gifts. The relationship between any parent and each child is unique. Every family member's personal experiences help forge the bonds with each mother, father, child, or sibling. No two people in any family will interpret single events or upbringings in the same way. This is not a bad thing, but it can be exasperating, because your spouse or child may disagree with every conclusion you've drawn from "that event that night," or "what really happened that year."

Let me share happenings that helped me gain insight into my daughters' lives, or that forced me to examine my own. It is obvious to me today that my diagnosis had greatly affected both of my girls at an early age. At the time, I may have been too busy to notice. I hope I wasn't intentionally blind to it.

Experts tell us much of our personality is hardwired before we are even born. Caitlin entered this world with a sunny disposition, a social butterfly able to power through adversity with a smile, traits she still exemplifies in her mid-twenties. I smile as I recall Caitlin's similar reaction to two events during her childhood, the first a strong earthquake that had awoken our family in the middle of the night, and the second when our SUV had spun and slid off an icy road while crossing the Coast Range in winter: *"Wow, that was fun!"*

When Caitlin was in sixth grade, she decided to join the track and field team at St. Pius X School. In the middle of the season, one of her coaches signed her up for the mile run, even though she had probably never run further than a slow lap or two around the school's grassy perimeter. I wasn't aware she would be competing in the event until I arrived at the meet.

The gun sounded and as her race progressed, Caitlin fell further and further behind the pack, clutching her side and, with tears in her eyes, crying out "Daddy, it hurts, it hurts" every time she passed me. I jogged along with her for a short stretch and told her she could stop, that it was okay to exit the race.

Instead, she continued crying but refused to quit running. When she crossed the finish line, she received thunderous applause from the stands and the other athletes on the field. She finished at least two minutes behind the rest of the runners, but I had never been prouder of her. That stick-to-it attitude still shines through in everything she does.

During high school, Caitlin was afflicted with a very aggressive form of acne; it covered her face with welts and was immune to most remedies. She ultimately got prescribed Accutane, the most powerful (and riskiest) acne medicine her dermatologist could prescribe. Initially, it worsened her condition, turning her face a darker shade of red, swelling her joints, and causing her body to ache all over. The weight of sheets and blankets at night were painful against her skin.

High school tends to draw out our insecurities. Caitlin grew embarrassed while having to deal with the public scrutiny and occasional harsh insults from other students. As the weeks of worsening acne turned into months, I remember walking into our kitchen in the middle of the night, seeking a cup of coffee to boost me while I continued working on a business presentation. Looking upstairs, I noticed a bright beam shooting through the bottom gap of a bathroom door. The light remained on after I had poured cream into my cup of fresh brew. The previous evening, Karen had found Caitlin sitting cross-legged on the bathroom counter and wrapped in a blanket, her face inches from the mirror, her eyes swollen, red, and wet. I wondered if she was again studying her damaged skin, begging for her condition to improve. I called upstairs and could sense the weight of the world as she walked to her room and said good night. I told her I loved her, that I was proud of her. Then I silently lashed out: *When the hell was this damn medicine going to start working?*

The medicine did eventually work, like magic. Her skin is flawless today. What is remarkable to me is that during all the hardship related to her skin condition, Caitlin remained publicly upbeat and optimistic. I'm still impressed by how she endured such a difficult adolescent experience, at a time when young girls are particularly sensitive about their looks and fitting in. Little Miss Sunshine had persevered.

Years later, I learned that our little optimist had struggled with my multiple sclerosis, and the way it had encroached on our family's future.

Excerpts of Caitlin's high school speech:

When I was a little girl, I thought of my Dad as Superman. He had a fairly demanding job at Intel and he wasn't around much during the day. At the time, this didn't bother me because I was at school all day, played sports in the afternoon, and in my eyes he was always there when it really mattered. Every night when he came home from work, he would run upstairs to my bedroom and sing "Here Comes the Sun" to me until I fell asleep. As I grew older I still loved the soothing tone of his voice to that Beatles song that I knew so well. He taught me to love all rock 'n' roll music. He taught me to dance, even when there was no music. But most importantly, my father has taught me to see God in all things.

My Dad has Primary Progressive Multiple Sclerosis. His disease has always frightened me and, to some extent, it always will. It has been an immense struggle for me to cope with his condition. My sophomore year my Dad fell in our garage, shattering his hip and breaking several bones. I heard him helplessly yelling and begging for my family to stay inside the house, for fear of his children seeing him in such a vulnerable state. I stood motionless in front of the door, terrified to move. I immediately shut my eyes in a hopeful attempt to shut out the rest of the chaotic world around me. Neighbors ran breathless to the house, ambulance sirens blared, and I stood, frozen in desperation.

I spent hours lost in my Dad's hospital room, hours that he doesn't even remember. Every day after school, my Brother would drive over to the hospital and we would do our homework together on the floor. It began to feel like I never left that hospital. I had dreams where I would be walking in the empty halls and they would never end. I started to shut down, I couldn't talk to my Mom, I couldn't talk to my friends, I couldn't talk to anyone but my older Brother. I thought that the pain associated with that night would prevent me from ever being able to relive it. I resented God and was constantly angry with Him.

I found myself avoiding the entire ordeal which, in the end, wounded me.

Then my Mom was diagnosed with possible Breast Cancer [it turned out to be Stage 0, and was followed by a lumpectomy and five years of Tamoxifen, a low-grade chemotherapy drug], I felt like my world was falling apart and, in reality, my faith was. My grades dipped, especially in my religion classes, which I saw as a complete joke and a waste of time and effort. My Catholic education from Kindergarten to Eighth grade meant nothing to me. In my mind God was nowhere to be found, and He certainly wasn't looking out for me.

The night before my sixteenth birthday, my Brother asked me to go to the hospital to have dinner with my Dad and after much convincing, I reluctantly agreed. When we arrived, he grabbed my hand and instead of walking me to my Dad's room he led me toward the hospital chapel. Without offering an explanation, he walked through the small wooden doors and I followed right behind him. As I entered the half-packed chapel, I could see my Dad's wheelchair in the aisle next to the first pew. My Brother grabbed my hand and didn't say anything as he walked forward; and neither did I. At that moment, my eyes flooded with tears and all the pain that I had kept inside of me for so long flowed out. For the first time since the accident, I felt God, I knew He was there. I knew that He understood the pain I was going through and I knew He forgave me for dealing with my emotions in the wrong way.

I don't think anyone realizes how great their family is until they feel what it would be like without them. That mass was the most beautiful and meaningful that I had ever been to. After we left the chapel, after the rest of the night that I spent hugging my Dad and thanking my Brother, I promised myself to see God in all situations. After that night, I had a faith that couldn't be broken or shaken.

One month later, I was accepted to become a Sophomore Overnight Leader. I decided, upon much reflection, to talk about my experiences with my Dad. I was cloaked in self-doubt and hesitation when I was chosen to present my speech [about faith] to the entire group. Five minutes before speaking, I ran outside into the cold and asked God to help me. I needed Him then, I needed Him to guide me.

My hands were shaking as I attempted to seize a feeling of courageousness, but I cried. I cried reading line after line, knowing that the voice carrying throughout the silent room was not my own. I presented myself to each person, my most honest self. When I finished, I could not lift my eyes from the crumpled papers that lay in between my trembling fingers. I could hear the clapping, yelling, and love that surrounded me.

During her junior year in college, Caitlin had grown totally uninspired by her studies and life's path. One day she stated she had made a huge mistake by not pursuing an art history degree. She felt obligated to continue down the road she had chosen (journalism), knowing that changing her degree would likely mean she could not graduate in four years (hence, cost her parents too much money). She also informed us that some of her peers considered art history a worthless degree to pursue (how typically American, I thought). We told her she needed to follow her truest calling, which we all agreed was clearly something in the arts. "But what will I do for a job?" she asked us. It will all work out, we advised.

She changed her major and enrolled in an art history study abroad program through Gonzaga University in Florence, Italy. She met a professor while there, Mercedes Carrara, who urged her to dream big and to set her goals higher as she pursued a career in the arts industry. That advice and boost of confidence helped change her life.

Caitlin sought out and was rewarded with internships at art auction houses Lyon & Turnbull, in Edinburgh, and Sotheby's, in London, the summer before her senior year at Oregon. After three years working for a regional auction house in Chicago, she has secured a position with Sotheby's in New York City. She moves east in two weeks.

New York is the pulse of the arts for America. Many of the world's most cherished works are housed in museums located throughout the city. Caitlin will be surrounded by millennia of historic art that she's fervent about. She'll be living her dream.

CHAPTER 19

Passion and Purpose

*Sometimes, as a parent, there's a chasm separating
who we are from who we need to be.*

Bre, b. 1992

B RE WAS BORN with a strong personality and a sense of
purpose. Karen and I have a wonderful memory of our
youngest child at three years old. She had been creating
a scene downstairs and needed some disciplining; Bre was quite
the debater even then. I eventually stood, pointed up the stairs
toward her bedroom, and told her to go to her room.

She threw a fit and was crying and shrieking at us as she
stomped up the stairs melodramatically, creating as much
commotion as possible. When she got to her room, she slammed
the door behind her with more force than I thought a small
child could muster. Soon we heard the door swing back open
and crash into the wall, followed by Bre stepping to the railing
to continue her tirade. She was hyperventilating as she shouted,
"I just want you to know," sob, sob, sob, "I went to my room
because I wanted to! Not because you told me to!" That was
followed by another thundering crash of the door.

Three years old!

Out of her sight in the family room downstairs, I gazed at Karen while shaking my head in astonishment, smiling. Bre has managed to harness that energy and it's become just one trait that makes her special today.

Many parents have at least one family member reminiscence that instantly prompts a dreadful unease. We have several such recollections, one of them involving Bre.

When a family moves to Oregon, there are many lifestyle adjustments that must be made. One piece of advice Oregonians give out-of-staters visiting the Oregon Coast is "be wary of sneaker waves," which roll in sporadically and are much larger than other breakers. In 1994, when Bre was two years old, our family was enjoying a sunny spring day on the beaches of Pacific City. I coaxed Bre into walking out into six to twelve inches of gentle surf. She was hesitant because I had moved her from the relative warmth of dry beach sand into the cold waters of the northern Pacific. Otherwise, there was nothing to be concerned about; the surf was calm and the situation was very much in my control.

I was ignorant to the dangers.

As Karen was filming father and daughter stepping through the shallow tides, a sneaker wave roared toward us while our backs were turned, crashing over our bodies. I should have been able to safely maintain my grasp, but my weaker "MS hand" did not respond the way my right side would have. As I heard and felt the wave breaking over us from behind, Bre got pulled from my grip.

I was overtaken by a five- to six-foot surge with significant amounts of foam and bubbles along the surface. I lost sight of her. Should I look in front of me? Has she been swept forward or back out to sea? I was instantly numbed by the gut-wrenching possibilities of what might be unraveling.

Watching the drama real-time through the eye of her video recorder, Karen dropped the camera and sprinted toward us. We have footage of flashing sky, sand, and water as she is running with the camera bouncing from around her neck.

I scanned the tides, restraining my panic. Bre was tiny and I knew it would be difficult to find her, but failing—*losing my daughter to the sea!*—was an unbearable thought.

Look quickly, carefully, instinctively.

I glanced ten feet to my left and thought I caught a flash of something rolling under the retreating foamy blue-green surge. Please let this be my little girl.

I rushed forward through the now waist-high water and clutched the spinning object. It was Bre. I am disturbed as I remind myself of the price of failure. But I found her.

The entire event lasted only thirty seconds, but it came close to being the proverbial *parents' worst nightmare.* The northwestern Pacific Ocean can be terribly unforgiving; we sometimes read about its casualties locally. Take a moment to let thirty seconds tick by while imagining you're standing in four feet of retreating surf, and your two-year-old daughter is gasping for air in front of, behind, or to the side of you. You must guess quickly and correctly. Or else.

Unpleasant, isn't it?

Excerpts from a blog post by Bre, 2015:

How My Dad's Disease Changed Me

Lately I've had the urge to open up about something I've never explored fully in writing before. My dad has Primary Progressive Multiple Sclerosis. For those of you who didn't watch the TV show *House*, MS is "a chronic, typically progressive disease involving damage to the sheaths of nerve cells in the brain and spinal cord, whose symptoms may include numbness, impairment of speech and of muscular coordination, blurred vision, and severe fatigue." I'm much too lazy to write up my own definition, and to be honest, I don't enjoy reading up on MS. There's a lot of scary shit out there on the Internet and I simply don't have the emotional capacity to read it all. Unsurprisingly, I've found that there isn't any definition of MS (or any disease, I'd wager) that can properly express what it is. Chronic illness is so complex and powerful. It will inevitably shape you, make you suffer, and enlighten you in ways that you may have never thought possible.

My very first memory sheds some light on this. I was around four or five years old, and my parents had just picked me up from Sunday School. I can vividly recall walking out of the building. I was on the right, a small figure next to my mom and dad. Someone held my hand. Maybe both of them did. My mom spoke with intention, and I somehow knew that what she was telling me was important, even critical, to my life. "Your dad has MS," she explained. She tried to relay to me what it all meant, what I could expect. How she did this for a five-year-old, I don't know. That moment has left an imprint upon me for my entire life. In my mind, there is no memory before it. Only after.

I can barely remember my dad ever walking.

That's a fact, but it doesn't make the sentence any less scary. I remember one particular experience with my dad and sister when I was around seven. We were at the beach and decided to explore an overgrown path full of ripe blackberries that wound down to a nearby river. I remember the blue jeans he wore, undeniably Levi's, and the way the denim moved across his legs as he placed one foot in front of the other. Even as a little girl, I possessed the quiet knowledge that these moments were important. My dad wanted us to see him walk while he could.

As I grew up, I witnessed my dad's health deteriorate. It happened at once slowly and suddenly. In the early days, he began using a cane to help support himself. A cane was no big deal to us kids. He had quite a few, though I don't believe he liked using any of them. His disease was just beginning to snake its way into the rest of his life; taking up space that he hadn't accounted for. Then one day, after participating in a medical study for a new MS drug, he stepped out of the car and crashed down onto the concrete floor of our garage. I must have been up in my room doing homework, because I didn't hear a thing. It wasn't until later that I began to absorb the gravity of what had happened. He had shattered his hip. When the ambulance came, the paramedics loaded him onto a stretcher—my dad, on a stretcher—and sped away into the dusk. As the saying goes, things get worse before they get better.

As a girl, Bre's relationship with me wasn't very different from those I had with her two siblings. Things began to change during her later teenage years and into college; I consider it a dark phase that was unnecessary and remains regrettable. I viewed the world as black-and-white for too much of my life, and I accordingly held strong opinions about how children should act and treat their parents. I demanded what I considered a modicum of respect. She pushed back on my expectations, and the divide grew wider.

Here are Bre's blogged reflections on living with a struggling father, and dealing with the added burdens of our now-strained relationship:

> I spent much of my adolescence brooding about my dad's disease. I had no idea how to manage his ailing health while maintaining a normal teenage life. In addition to the tumult and angst that defines high school, my dad was nearly unable to make it across the living room using a walker. We butted heads about everything from politics to my poor manners. I was outspoken and unrelenting in my viewpoints. Defiance is part of my nature, and I wasn't afraid to let him know it. More than that, I experienced an immense amount of pressure during this time. I fought what felt like day and night to make my parents proud, yet constantly felt as though I was failing to measure up. My dad and I would engage in our habitual arguments, and afterwards I would head up to my room and weep into a pillow until, finally, I stopped. I confessed these moments to no one, and quietly, as if a whisper in our house, I suffered.

It is unacceptable that I allowed the bond with my youngest child to weaken due to such rigid demands for conformity. Yes, I was fatigued from disease during the darkest phases of our discord, but it would be wrong for me to blame my behavior on poor health. In truth, I had much to learn about unconditional love.

In Bre's mind view, I had become too strict, disinterested in her life, and poorly understood who she was or who she could become. Perhaps that was true; I hope it wasn't.

As with all of us, her perspectives were her realities, so any suggestions that she might have been mistaken about me or my intentions were met with derision. But beyond all the turmoil and emotions, the only thing that really mattered was that my grown-up little girl was injured by my judgments.

During the peak of my dismay with Bre's attitude, during her junior year in college, Karen warned me that if I didn't change the way I was interacting with Bre, I'd lose my daughter. Those were very close to her exact words. Karen read an email I was intending to send to Bre, calling her out for what I had concluded were unacceptable behaviors. I signed the message, "I love you."

Karen insisted I was unnecessarily poisoning my future with Bre. I pushed back on my wife, asking how she could dare accuse a loving father, who was only trying to teach his child respect, of such destructive parenting. Karen told me Bre and I were stubborn, that we had each dug in to defend our positions. She said I needed to retreat, not to confront, insisting that mixing damning judgment with a message that ends "I love you" was ineffective and hurtful. I deleted the entire message, minus the last three words.

I began to take similar courses of action in all my communications with Bre. Soon thereafter, our relationship slowly improved, then dramatically. I am disheartened by how I let the tensions between us obscure the essence of a wonderful young lady, a daughter I admire in countless ways. My life has often been about difficult lessons.

Bre's blog continued:

All my life, people have been deeply inspired by my dad. That includes me. In the darkest moments of our relationship, which was often overshadowed by his disease, I was always struck by his optimism and faith. He was born to overcome this obstacle, and it's because of his unmistakable grace and resilience that I am able to endure it myself. In the past two years, my dad and I have completely transformed our relationship. In turn, my relationship to his disease has changed as well.

I'm just now beginning to take ownership of the pain his MS caused me and its unavoidable place in my life. I can't hide from it, so I face it head on, with all of my courage and love. Today, I'm beyond thankful for my dad, who has become a close confidante for me. I often call him on a whim to solicit some advice or update him on my career. There is an unspoken depth to the bond between us that makes it very special. He's currently writing a memoir about his life, which includes a touching chapter about daughters. He recently rewrote his entire piece about our own relationship and sent it to me for feedback. 'Is this honest?' he was trying to ask. It was so humanizing and vulnerable. Much of what he wrote neither of us have said out loud to each other . . . yet. It was through writing that my dad began to reclaim himself amid his hardships. Our childhood house is now his haven for writing; an undertaking that requires only the most beautiful part of him: his mind. Interestingly, both of us find solace through writing. Perhaps it's through this shared passion that we can examine how we've been broken, and build something better of ourselves. I am my father's daughter.

After Bre graduated, she moved home to begin her job search. Initially, she pursued employment with little input from me. Soon she began discussing job options, and more importantly, the deepest passions she had in life: human rights, sustainability, fashion, and design. The longer we talked, the more I listened, the more I began to understand what made her tick, the stronger our bonds continued to grow. We discovered we had much more in common than whatever we had disagreed about.

The solutions to our family tensions are often staring us in the face—we just need to open our eyes, scrap some of our lectures, and tell the other person only that we love them, without qualifications. *And live it.* Should I have discovered the road to reconciliation with Bre earlier? Of course. But such things don't always come easily. Every relationship in any family has a unique set of dynamics affecting it. All our personalities are distinctive. And sometimes the obvious isn't so obvious. At least, as you've just discovered, it wasn't always to me.

Bre has developed an even stronger commitment to human rights and making the world a better place. A service trip to Ecuador opened her eyes in ways that living among the socio-economically disadvantaged can. After studying abroad in Angers, France, she secured an internship as an eco-fashion editor for a web start-up in London, Urban Times. It didn't surprise me she had been offered the position, or that she had organized her transition to London, including the negotiation of a flat to live in, with minimal help from her parents. She's passionate, capable, and ambitious.

After three years working at Nike, Bre recently moved from Portland to Austin, Texas, to work for Outdoor Voices, a fast-growing recreational apparel company. With her departure, Karen and I now have children living in New York, Texas, and Southern California. As parents we worked hard to give our children wings, not fully internalizing they all might fly away.

*   *   *

Having reflected on each of our children's writings, I am struck by how much more wisdom they possessed than I did during the teen years and beyond. They certainly had more empathy, sympathy, and understanding of life's challenges.

Growing up in families touched by chronic illnesses will somehow affect the entire household. It appears to me Ken, Caitlin, and Bre understand that no family is immune from sickness and tragedy, and that faith in ourselves, those we love, and God can help deliver us from sadness or misery prompted by any misfortune.

CHAPTER 20

The Last Times

Ordinary moments grow profound in retrospect.

EVERY MSER WHOSE life has been significantly encumbered by their disease holds a mental list of The Last Times. The last time he drove a car. The last time he walked. The last time he worked.

The last time I walked any distance unaided was in Pacific City, Oregon, over fifteen years ago. I remember crossing Cape Kiwanda Drive holding Bre's hand; she was eight years old. Five years earlier, a sneaker wave had ripped her from my grip in the same seaside community, nearly stealing her from us. But this Oregon Coast day was splendid: seventy-something degrees, blue skies, and a slight breeze. We walked on black asphalt paths meandering through tall beach grass, pines, and dunes. About ten minutes into our stroll, my legs grew heavy and I began wondering if I could make it back to our home. That weighty sensation never fully abated; my legs had forever transformed. Regardless, my walk with Bre was perfect and is forever entrenched in my mind.

Caitlin and I shared our last dance her junior year during the Jesuit High Father-Daughter Event. I carried my cane onto the floor as a precaution, and I can clearly recall the smile on her face as we moved in a slow circular pattern. I spent most of my time that night talking with other fathers whose names I would be hard-pressed to recall; I was too focused on appreciating the special moment with my daughter, and I smile at the flashback images of her floating about the room like the social butterfly she was (and is). She later handed me a long-stemmed red rose, a ceremonious finale to the evening. I silently accepted that the experience on that dance floor would be impossible to repeat at the following year's event.

The last time Ken and I spent the day on the Nestucca Delta, dropping crab pots and rings in pursuit of keeper-sized Dungeness crabs, he was a high schooler. There were days when the two of us would land over thirty large, hard-shelled Dungies. It was special just hanging out on the Boston Whaler, setting the traps, and steering onto a sandbar for some snacks and idle time. Ken would explore the driftwood, shells, and dead creatures lining the beaches and river's edge. We'd catch enough meat for several meals, sometimes trading portions of our crab for lingcod or geoduck clams our beach friends had fished and hunted for. Other times we would all combine our catches and enjoy a neighborhood seafood extravaganza, feasting for hours.

I can't remember the last time Karen and I walked hand-in-hand; I've been trying but failing to picture the specific day and moment. I know the last time we dined out together, minus my scooter or wheelchair, was at the Portland City Grill, a favorite restaurant of ours with views of Mt. Hood, Mt. Saint Helens, and the city. That was over ten years ago.

I can vividly picture the final time I drove. I was backing up in our driveway when my right foot pressed against the gas and brake pedals simultaneously, creating the nightmarish situation that could have resulted in me pinning Caitlin into the side of our garage. I never drove again.

My life with chronic disease is all about perspective. While many of the Last Time recollections are ingrained, important memories are being created during what I call my gimpy years (the last ten). I now take "walks" with Karen in my wheelchair during the summer and late fall. We continue to have romantic dinners at the Portland City Grill. Sometimes we'll stop at Piazza Italia or Gallo Nero before or after appointments downtown, enjoying the sunshine and amazing food on sidewalk tables.

It's true, I can't dance anymore, but if there's one thing I was never known for (or more accurately, that I was *infamous* for), it was my dancing. It's quite possible the healthy Ken Cruickshank permanently scarred his girls with his public moves on the dance floor (I hope I did). Nowadays, dances and walks with my daughters on a beautiful Oregon day have been replaced by fireside chats, a nice pinot noir or cabernet sauvignon, and some extra-dark chocolates. Looks to me like the girls and I may have traded up!

While Ken and I no longer fly float planes to Bamfield, British Columbia, for several days of salmon and halibut fishing, we've figured out other ways to travel and enjoy magical moments. We attended the 2011 NCAA BCS National Championship Game between Oregon and Auburn, in Arizona. It was an amazing experience, even though the Ducks did lose in heartbreaking fashion.

The list of lifestyle adjustments dictated by my disease continues to grow. Typically, the forced transitions are gradual, mimicking the progression of the demyelination of my nerves. Sometimes they are immediate, such as when I made the decision to permanently stop driving. But as any MSer's disease evolves, so can the ways in which he ensures his life remains fulfilling, with great optimism for the future. It does no good to fret about mandatory changes to one's familiar routines.

And anyway, whether one is healthy or affected by chronic illness, the only constant in all our lives is change.

CHAPTER 21

Misery Loves Company

Sometimes the silver lining is a funny story.

S PEAKING OF LAST Time experiences, this was another (it better have been).

If my proctologist Dr. Grunkemeier ever calls to schedule my five-year follow-up colonoscopy, *I am not home*. The esteemed doctor is in fact a gastroenterologist, but proctologist sounds appropriately more villainous.

For several years, Karen had been urging me to schedule a colonoscopy to ensure I was, minus that MS thing, super healthy. I had never gotten around to making the appointment. Truth be told, I had *no intention* of ever getting around to it. One day, Karen flashed me a wide smirk and stated she had scheduled two colonoscopy procedures back to back, one for each of us lucky spouses. Oh yes, I felt deceived, but worse—I was trapped. Of course, I also knew, not so deep down, it was likely prudent to get this dreaded Roto-Rooter job off the to-do list.

Karen was only forty-five years old at the time; most doctors wouldn't have recommended the procedure until she had hit fifty. However, we have perhaps the best GP on earth, and he had recently read a French health study concluding there was a correlation between breast cancer (Karen's had been caught pre-stage 1) and colon cancer, which now justified my wife's colonoscopy at her early age.

Dr. Grunkemeier, Karen, and I were seated in his office and he explained what a colonoscopy entailed and how we would need to "prep." Whenever the words *colonoscopy* and *prep* are intermingled within the same sentence, people tend to nod knowingly as their lips form into a devilish grin. While being presented the manner of our prep, Karen took the liberty to inform him that one of the side effects of my MS was occasionally getting constipated. I felt slightly violated— isn't that a topic of discussion *I* should control? He commented that he and I shared the condition (let's all just talk about constipation), and he doesn't even have multiple sclerosis. Imagine that. I couldn't wait to thank Karen for enlivening our discussion.

Dr. Grunkemeier, being a respected professional totally unconcerned about any protesting drivel from the man in the scooter, had decided that, to ensure my body would be good and ready for the day of reckoning, he was going to double the amount of liquids and laxatives I was to consume beginning two and a half days prior to the exam. Karen was prescribed one container of MiraLax and sixty-four ounces of Gatorade, plus some crazy amount of water. I got prescribed *128 ounces of Gatorade, two containers of MiraLax,* and *double the crazy amount of water* Karen had been prescribed—*plus Duculax tablets*!

I will advise you right now to never simultaneously consume multiple products with the letters *L, A,* or *X* anywhere in their brand names. To spook me further, the good doctor informed us that the evening prior to C-Day, we were supposed to wake up every few hours to consume volumes of said liquids.

Understand, if an MSer does not get his sleep, his body may not function properly. This colonoscopy thing was setting up to be one very interesting experiment.

I followed the doctor's directions to a T, because I'm a mature adult patient (or, because Karen was eying me like a hawk). I drank and drank and drank. I had to "go" more than usual, but not excessively so. I began to wonder where the heck all this water and Gatorade was going.

Being deprived of a good night's rest meant I was miserable after I had awoken to dress for transportation to the happy clinic where my bottom would be scoped. As I stood in front of my washbasin and mirror in our master bathroom, naked as a jaybird, I bent over to set my elbows on the counter to brush my teeth.

Something shot out of my rear.

I was an unhappy mixture of groggy, overmedicated, surprised, and annoyed. I twisted around to find a clearish liquid (Gatorade) on our light carpet. Karen hadn't yet noticed and I was so peeved about having to prepare for this C-thing that I decided to nonchalantly continue brushing my teeth.

Insanity can be defined as doing the same thing over and over and expecting a different result. I bent forward to put my elbows on the counter *three different times*, almost as if it had been preordained that I must do so, and *all three times* Gatorade shot from the aft portal of my body.

I eventually decided to let Karen in on my little secret. "There's some Gatorade on the floor." There was no reaction so I added some detail. "It shot out of my butt."

She turned around from her vanity on the other side of our bathroom and snapped back, "You've got to be kidding me." Karen had also been deprived of a solid slumber. She was in no mood for yours truly to complicate C-Day.

"Nope. Right there. Let's deal with it when we get back. It's just Gatorade." I wasn't going to let The Inglorious Event dictate the terms of our morning, darn it. We can leave the orange liquid right where it is until we're good and ready to get the carpet cleaner fired up—*after* our colonoscopies.

"Are you serious? No way. It came out of your butt! I'm not going to leave it on the carpet; that's absurd."

"Karen, leave it alone. Okay? Let's just get to the clinic and get this stupid thing—*this thing you scheduled*—over with. By the way, I'm never doing this again."

"Oh, grow up. What a dumb thing to say. Just get out of the way so I can clean this up." She wasn't about to leave the carpet alone.

"But Karen!"

"Just get your stuff and wait for me in the kitchen. I can't believe you thought I'd leave it there. Asinine." The general had spoken.

I mumbled something incoherently, just as I was bending down to be seated in my electric wheelchair. You guessed it—Gatorade shoots onto the seat as I am dropping into position. I was now sitting in a fluid my wife liked to tell me was shot out of my butt. I grumbled something else and proceeded to depart. As I was rolling out of the room, I twisted my neck for one final dissent, "*It's just Gatorade!*"

How was I going to make it to the clinic if fluid exited my body every time I stood, sat, or bent? I had visions of spraying my "prep" everywhere while waiting in the reception area of the house of horrors. C-Day was off to a lousy start. Just then, Ken, our transportation to and from the medical facility, strolled downstairs.

Because my brain had shrunk overnight, I stood up to take a sip of coffee while greeting him. More orange stuff shot out of my keester. I was exhausted and enraged. I was also delirious. I asked Ken if he could grab a couple of towels, one to wipe off my wheelchair, the other to fold up and lay in my shorts like a big *man diaper*.

Ken strolled back into the room and was about to wipe his father's Gatorade-tinged buttocks before I told him, "No, I'll take care of that." He was going to fix the old man up! I will never forget that.

Karen had finished carpet cleaning the "stuff that came out of your butt" and the three of us merrily proceeded to the building where doctors with probes eagerly awaited their adequately prepped and miserable patients.

After we had been checked in, I was undressed, put into a hospital gown, and seated on the edge of a portable bed. I suddenly felt an intense pressure building within me. More specifically, within the area a colonoscopy device was soon to be inserted.

"Excuse me, nurse, I think I am about to explode. I don't want to drain out all over this bed, so can you help me get to the restroom?" I am sure Karen was happy to have already been taken to her own changing room in preparation of the main event. She no longer had to deal with the leaky and irritable husband. The nurse got me to a toilet and I was totally unfazed sitting in front of her. Wretchedness removes our inhibitions.

Right then, the spigot that was my bottom was opened and I began to drain . . . and drain . . . and drain. While departing, the nurse smiled and said, "Wow." Defeated, I gazed back at her and replied, "Yeah, no kidding." I added, "It's Gatorade." She shut the door and I am guessing another one thousand ounces of famous sports drink geysered from my body.

Perhaps you're reading this and saying to yourself, "Mr. Book Writer, I am tired of hearing about your draining bottom; please move on to a more salient point. Stop feeling sorry for yourself."

Herein lies the irony and the lesson learned. Karen had to schedule back-to-back colonoscopies to get her reluctant husband committed to the procedure. But as I was lying on a bed after my exam, I heard our doctor, in a separate room, tell my wife, "You've dodged a bullet." Karen had a large, aggressive tumor growing inside her colon, one Dr. Grunkemeier believed was likely to have become cancerous. He had already removed it. Karen's three-year follow-up procedure showed no new tumors. This is why, despite all the unpleasantries associated with the feared examination, and despite the myriad excuses we can all craft, getting a colonoscopy simply makes a lot of sense.

My only recommendation is this: If you have multiple sclerosis, beg your spouses not to inform your doctors that you sometimes get constipated. Otherwise, you may be prescribed wicked double doses of Gatorade, MiraLax, Duculax, water—and who knows what else. I hope you're paying attention, my MS brethren.

After rereading this chapter's narrative, I've respectfully decided to stop calling Dr. Grunkemeier a proctologist.

CHAPTER 22

Dodging Bullets

Who are those guys with sunglasses in the bushes?

I F ANYONE DESERVED a special fiftieth birthday celebration, it was Karen.

I asked her, "What would you like for your big day, if you could have anything?" She didn't hesitate. "I would love to walk down to Cecilia and John's (my sister and brother-in-law) dock and dive into the warm Caribbean on the morning of my birthday." She quickly added, as I knew she would: "No, we can't do that this year; it's too expensive."

She was largely correct; it was not the best year to be spending money on big vacations; the airfares alone would be painful. But I couldn't wait for her to finish listing all the reasons why we *shouldn't* travel to her favorite island, because I also had a strong opinion: "Stop. We're going to St. Croix." I called Cecilia and John the next day to inquire about visiting their waterfront home for Karen's birthday at Christmastime; they insisted that we come. We all began dreaming of sun, seafood, and slumber.

Traveling with advanced MS to St. Croix, or any other faraway destination, requires lots of preparation. Take man diapers, for instance. I bought some several years ago, due to frightful anticipations of having *to go* while midair, where it would be extraordinarily difficult to get to the bathroom without my walker. I wanted an alternative to drenching my pants, of concealing a potential coffee-went-through-me moment. Good news: It turns out that just wearing the absorbent skivvies calms my anxieties so well that I haven't had to "use" them even once. Way to go, man diapers! (Available at Costco.)

Owing to their work schedules in 2012, Caitlin and Karen had planned on flying together to meet up with Bre and me in St. Croix. Bre was entering her senior year at Oregon and had volunteered to escort me to the Virgin Islands. In order to acclimate to Eastern Standard Time for a few days before departing for our final destination, Bre and I stopped in Georgia. We rested at Good Buddy Ron's place in La Grange, recharged my body's batteries (the routine up to, during, and after even a short flight wipes me out for at least a day), before flying nonstop into St. Croix. Completing both legs (Portland to Atlanta, Atlanta to St. Croix) in one day would have ruined my vacation—I'd have been wiped out for a week upon arrival.

In anticipation of our visit, Ron had a ramp custom-built that began at his driveway, slanted upward over several stone steps, and delivered me and my portable scooter onto a curved entryway leading into his home. I traveled up and down this wooden path several times during our first two days there, without any problems. My fifth attempt was nearly a disaster.

As I was halfway down the sloping ramp, with my head about six feet above the patio cement below me, I slowed the scooter down for no specific reason. The change in speed shifted my weight and I began to tilt off the ramp and to the right, freefalling toward the concrete.

The last time I had fallen onto cement, I ended up in the hospital for weeks. But this imminent injury was going to be far worse; I knew it. Anticipating the force of my crash onto the unforgiving surface, my thoughts shifted to Bre, who was walking contentedly ten to fifteen feet ahead of me. This is what flashed through my mind: *But she's already seen me fall too many times!* And now she might be witness to something catastrophic, something life-changing . . . or life-ending. That isn't melodrama. The result of a fall from that height, either sideways or headfirst, would have been at best a shattered arm or shoulder, and at worst a busted skull and broken neck. It would have ruined our St. Croix celebration of Karen's fiftieth. It would have scarred Bre forever.

Good Buddy Ron saved the day! Without my paying attention, Ron had been walking along the right side of the ramp as I was descending, a step or two behind me. When he realized I was tipping over the edge of the ramp, he leapt forward and caught the human sack of potatoes. As I fall, I am completely dead weight, with little ability to affect the manner of my collapse, so he had to clutch and control two hundred pounds of limp Ken.

Because of the layout of his patio, there was no place for him to set me down, and only a narrow path to maneuver both of our bodies. Bre quickly moved my scooter to clear space. Ron was struggling and I was unable to offer any help; my limbs were wet noodles as he carried me toward my scooter and set me down. Disaster averted.

The reality is, not only would I have ruined *our* family's holiday vacation, but probably Ron's family's Christmas break, as well. I'd have been hospitalized in Atlanta for God knows how long, and he wouldn't have left town for his scheduled skiing vacation in Lake Tahoe, because that's the kind of friend he is.

After the near miss, we drove to Auburn, Alabama, for a great dinner next to the campus of the 2011 BCS national champions in football. Ron's Auburn-rabid wife, Julie, took a photo of me dressed up in my adopted University of Oregon regalia—the team Auburn had beat in the championship—in front of an

Auburn University mural. The photo was framed and placed on the kitchen counter before I rolled in for breakfast the following morning. Southerners take their college football very, very seriously. *Go War Eagles!*

Bre and I left Atlanta for St. Croix two days later, meeting up with the rest of our family. Karen's fiftieth turned out to be everything she (and thus I) had hoped for. She awakened on the morning of her birthday, strolled down to Cecilia's new dock, gazed out to the sea and Buck Island, and proceeded to dive in—just as she had dreamt about. The next day, Karen swam to Buck Island! Almost two miles of water! With nothing but goggles! *I was not happy.*

For several days, Coast Guard helicopters had been flying past, and hovering over, my sister's dock. Cecilia grew annoyed, assuming some muckety-mucks in the local Island government were investigating whether she had built the dock to code— which she had. Whenever a helicopter would begin another pass, she would storm out of the house and point accusingly at its occupants, with a forearm recently encased in a plaster cast resulting from a broken wrist. I was entertained by her enthusiastic responses to the commotion. *You go, girl!*

We soon learned that the men in the helicopter were Secret Service agents studying the layout of the water, beach, and surrounding lands in advance of Joe Biden's St. Croix vacation. The vice president and his wife, Jill, stayed right next door to us for about a week. The agents would occasionally pop out of the bushes as we approached the dock and property lines. They would rotate shifts covering the perimeter of the famous couple's vacation rental—each of them looking very capable of doing an excellent job of protecting the Pennsylvanians.

One morning, Karen and Bre followed a seldom-used alternative route off my sister's lot, a road we shared with the owner of the Bidens' rental property. The ladies were stopped by the agents but declared they had a right to use the road. The men in black obliged after having bomb-sniffing dogs circle the vehicle. Very exciting.

That week, at the nearby Duggan's restaurant, a few of the agents were eating dinner at a table next to ours; they primarily just observed everything happening around them. We later discovered Vice President Biden had dined there, too, though we never saw him. The bodyguards had gotten used to seeing us relaxing and socializing on the beach property next to theirs, so when I stood to transfer to my scooter upon our departure, they offered to assist me. I told them, "No thanks, I've got it." I now regret that decision. It would have been fun to inform friends that on-duty Secret Service agents had lifted me onto my scooter. All through dinner, I had a tune from my youth embedded in my consciousness: *Secret Agent man, Secret Agent man . . .*

I decided to take a swim with Karen in our hosts' saltwater pool one afternoon. Karen was stroking laps as I allowed myself to slowly *timberrr* into the water after releasing my walker. Though it was only five feet deep at its deepest point, I was unable to stay upright. I had difficulty keeping my head above water, and I panicked. As I bobbed upward, breaking the surface, I yelled out, *"Help!"*

Karen had been trained as a lifeguard in her youth and knew exactly how to respond. She clutched me from behind, lifted me up, and guided me to the edge of the pool. The whole incident lasted maybe thirty seconds, but it was yet another reminder of how I needed to be more diligent about weighing risks.

Our St. Croix Christmas and fiftieth birthday celebrations were perfect. Cecilia and John surprised us with a special evening of dining, wine, and entertainment at the Buccaneer Resort on the evening of Karen's birthday. Each sunset, we enjoyed cocktails out on the dock with family and Cruzan (St.

Croix locals) acquaintances. I kept hoping the Bidens would traverse the sands to come and party with us, but they never did. With their busy schedules, I suspect they just wanted to be left alone for a few days. Too bad; they missed a good time.

I sometimes hesitate at the thought of any future travel adventures, but then I remind myself I never want MS to dictate too many of the terms of my life. We can't stop living; we can't stop dreaming. In fact, writing this chapter has stirred my travel bug. Karen and I need to get some dates on the calendar for a trip to . . .

PART IV
Strength and Wisdom

Unexpected revelations of life's greatest truths.

CHAPTER 23

Inspirations

Most of us are pretty darn fortunate.
Perspective is a gift.

I WAS NOT PHYSICALLY cured in Lourdes. I didn't leave my scooter at the grotto, inspiring others through the sight of my miracle. Catholics believe people have been cured of various afflictions at the shrine of Our Lady, but like most of the millions who visit annually, I was not mysteriously chosen for such graces. I am not saddened that I have arrived home still unable to walk, drive, or function independently. For, as is true with so many of those visiting the grotto where we believe the Blessed Mother Mary spoke to a young Bernadette Soubirous over 150 years ago, I left Lourdes a changed man.

I have scarred nerves in my brain and in my spine. The most threatening issues are the lesions in the nerve canal of my upper vertebrae. They sometimes appear as round marbles in an MRI image and are spaced about three-quarters of an inch apart. As the scarring of the myelin sheathes around my nerves continues to worsen, the transmissions from my brain to the rest of my body will be further hindered, affecting my legs, arms, fingers, and feet. Without some major breakthroughs in the science of MS, my symptoms may progress to a point where I will become bedridden. That situation would present a host of new challenges and risks.

If or when that happens, I will be okay.

My trip to Lourdes, as a guest of the Order of Malta[1], isn't the reason I know I will be able to handle the difficulties that may lie down the road; it only strengthened my resolve and reinforced that I can manage any dilemma placed before me. Anyone who's visited the shrine in Lourdes will tell you there is an otherworldly reverence and energy pervading the area. Mary suffered intensely during Jesus's final persecution and ultimate crucifixion; she surely has a special empathy for those of us who are struggling. The inspirations garnered from my pilgrimage were the result of interacting with others seeking support and courage for their own (more) difficult life journeys.

It is easy to be overcome with what we may see as our unfair burdens related to slowly incapacitating illnesses. But I am not the only person with deteriorating health. And I am fortunate; I have lived an active life for decades, despite MS. Consider the plight of parents whose children struggle with terrible sicknesses, like my niece and her husband. They were accompanied to Lourdes one year before our journey to France. Their daughter, Grace, is battling a rare genetic disorder[2] that has forever altered her life, and she's just a young child.

No, it isn't "fair" or "right" that these seemingly endless trials are placed at anyone's feet; life doesn't dole out burdens this way. But as adults, I believe the hardships we encounter can push us to become beacons of hope for ourselves, for our families, and for others. And through that, I think, we can become better, stronger, and more relevant.

While in Lourdes, I met people battling what seemed like every type of illness: chronic diseases, cancers, burns, strokes, birth defects—it's a long list. The stories of the ailing we met were often concurrently gut-wrenching and uplifting. There was genuine camaraderie among all of us *malades*, a special relatability.

Chris is an amazing young hero from San Diego whose legs were incinerated (and eventually lost) after he had stepped on an IED in Afghanistan and was, as he not so eloquently described it, "barbecued." He suffered horrifying burns over much of his body and underwent years of painful skin grafts, surgeries, and rehabilitation. Chris told Karen he was not special, and that he was glad it was him, and not the trailing soldiers under his command, who had stepped on the bomb. As their leader, he didn't want to have to call the families of multiple enlistees, telling them he hadn't done "his job," that he hadn't protected brothers, sons, or husbands. And Chris says he is not a hero? I am struck by his unselfishness and honor.

Cardinal Timothy Dolan delivered a sermon at a Mass attended by Chris and our group at the grotto. As one of the religious stated that day, the line between heaven and earth is very thin at Lourdes. Karen and I have a cherished photo of Cardinal Dolan embracing Chris as he sat in his wheelchair in front of the shrine with the statue of Mary in the background, which is placed precisely where Saint Bernadette is said to have conversed with the mother of Jesus for sixteen days. The expressions upon Chris's and Cardinal Dolan's face as they embrace display a level of compassion that appears not of this world.

Bryce is bound to a wheelchair with spastic arms and legs caused by a traumatic birth, but he can talk through an amazing technology that "reads" his eyes as he stares at a screen equipped with a speaker. This struggling body, a person often gazed at without much contemplation of his plight, is so much more than the twisting young man buckled into his chair. While in Lourdes, I sensed intelligence and awareness through his alert eyes. When he wasn't contorting from the spasms, during those brief periods of being uninhibited, I glimpsed the face of a handsome, quizzical young man. His burden is great.

During a meeting with the other *malades* from throughout the country, and after listening to the gripping stories people told relating to their illnesses and life journeys, Bryce's computer suddenly spoke: "I want to tell you all that I love you, and I love my family." And then he cried, uncontrollably. Others cried with him. Every person in the room could relate to an emotional release prompted by days, weeks, and years of constantly battling health issues that seemed terribly cruel in their relentless pursuits.

Jessica is a young lady from California who was also a guest of the Order of Malta on our trip to Lourdes. She had overcome bone cancer in each leg as a child and adolescent. As a senior at the University of Alabama, she detected lumps within the tissue of her breast. She ended up having to undergo a double mastectomy and had all her lymph nodes removed. As if that weren't enough pain and adversity for this magnetic young woman to confront, she was later advised she suffered from a genetic mutation that would predispose her to various cancers in the future (barring a medical breakthrough). And yet, through all the hurt and disappointment, she remains full of life with an unyielding level of faith and positivity. Faith in herself, faith in mankind, faith in God. She inspires.

Jessica is tall and fashionable with beautiful dark skin; she is, in fact, a model. The first time we met her, she was wearing a pink wig that flowed down her back (she'd lost her mane during chemo treatments). We were recently reunited with her when we flew to Southern California to visit my family and friends. I was excited to have Jessica and her mother meet our son and my family. My relatives were all duly impressed with the ailing young lady who handles her problems with such grace.

I observed Jessica bless herself and offer a silent prayer as the strangers around her were engaged in various conversations; I wished I could have intercepted her thoughts, so I could have offered up my own intentions in accordance with hers. Just months after our trip to the grotto, Jessica learned she had thyroid cancer (it was surgically removed and followed up with radiation in 2014). It is difficult to understand why such fine young people are forced to endure incredible suffering in their lives.

Lourdes helped put my struggles into perspective. I was moved by many of those we met there, and I hope to honor their valor by offering my own examples of coping with adversity while maintaining optimism for a fulfilling future.

I am sick, but I tell myself my difficulties are actually a gift. This was an elusive perspective for me to wrap my head around for many years. I have learned through my experiences, or by sharing time with others suffering from physical and mental diseases, that we ailing are special—certainly no better than anyone else, certainly not owed any specific privilege by our families or society. Rather, we are given the opportunity to offer up courage and hope in the face of illness or misfortune.

That might be a wonderful thing.

Yes, I get motivated by the likes of Chris, Bryce, and Jessica. And when I think of them, I recall another special young man who profoundly affected my life: Danny K.

Dying with Grace

I had been preparing for hip replacement surgery. My life was not in danger and the pain was nothing compared to my first accident, surgery, and therapy. I just wanted to focus on adjusting to my new titanium hardware and getting back home to my "normal" routine. Thus, I instructed Karen not to let anyone visit me in the hospital during the first week of my therapy. But on the second day of my stay, she informed me she had scheduled a visitor, and before I could object, she told me the visitor would be Danny K. I was instantly pacified.

Danny K is special to me and many others. When I pray at night, there are fifty-two departed souls whose names I utter (I sometimes joke to myself that when I can no longer recall the entire list, it'll be my time to go). I begin with my brother John (left us at age twenty-five), my father Richard (eighty-seven), my niece Sarah (eighteen), and my father-in-law Jack (seventy-eight). The other forty-eight names are fairly well aligned in the order of their deaths. Danny K is six names from the end of the list, and when I get to him, I pause to recite these words: "Danny K, who died with grace." Because that's exactly what he did.

Danny was a family friend who left us at age twenty, eventually succumbing to an aggressive bone cancer called Ewing's sarcoma. The young man epitomized goodness and gentleness through everything he said and did, before and after his diagnosis. He fought like heck to live, even when he knew he was going to die. And through all his incredible pain and difficult trials, he never complained, never said unkind things, and was always an inspiration to be around. I was deeply honored Danny K had asked Karen if he could see me in the hospital, so I immediately told her "absolutely." After visiting with me, Danny met with a doctor that same day, to decide whether to have one of his arms removed at the shoulder: His cancer had spread.

It can be a gift for those battling adversity to share their wisdom, fears, dreams, and consoling with other ailing persons. Each of us determines what manner and frequency of such interactions might help us most (or if at all). I get particularly inspired by people who have suffered greatly and yet express nothing but dignity and humble acceptance of their misfortune, redefining grace under pressure into grace in the face of unyielding pain or trials. They haven't surrendered hope—these same people are typically optimistic battlers until the very end. This is why I met with Danny K, to be awed by a fine young man who was carrying his cross so admirably.

Days before Danny K left this world, he was moved to a bed in his family's living room. Karen and I met with him one afternoon as his wilted body lay upon the sheets. I asked him if he was afraid to die, and if he believed Jesus would embrace him upon his passing. He looked at me and said he knew God and heaven were awaiting him. He told us he would miss his entire family, and that he especially appreciated the untiring commitment his mother had made to him during a difficult journey that was ending. He wasn't bitter or frightened as death approached his bedside; instead, he was impressed by, and thankful for, his family's and mother's love. Wow.

God bless you, Danny K.

CHAPTER 24

Seeking to Understand

*"Sometimes bad things just happen. It's God and our faith
that help get us through."*
—Agnelo Gomes, sfx

I DO NOT TRY to defend my convictions with an absolute
skeptic; any contentious debate would diminish the
integrity of my beliefs. I admire any person committed
to his or her religious doctrine in this complicated world we
inhabit, whatever faith that might be. I have friends of every
major religion, and a few who are staunch atheists.

God is prayed to each day and night by the fortunate, but also
by those seeking sanctuary from pain, disease, and calamity. The
reflections of those who are ailing may include these questions:
Why me? Did I deserve this?

I have never accepted that we are given miseries in life as
punishment for actions we've taken or decisions we've made.
While I believe God could exert His authority to present any
burden or blessing imaginable, I endorse the idea that some
people are simply less fortunate than others—their number
gets called. I hope any person of faith challenged by MS, ALS,
Parkinson's, or any other disease maintains a similar perspective.

We are not ill due to any retribution for doubts about God, or for sinfulness. If those were the benchmarks for being stricken by illness, every person on earth would be afflicted.

God is my path to accepting and coping with hardship. I consider it a profound comfort to call upon His infinite love and presence during periods of loneliness or despair. In my opinion, doubters who conclude that conviction in Him or His unyielding love for us is a crutch defying logic are obscuring something beautiful. That said, all of us doubt at times, even those things we ardently believe in.

It seems natural and essential to me that there would be a reality—a perfect virtue—that is so fantastic that much of it is beyond human comprehension. I want a reason greater than my humanity to help guide me through life with optimism and hope. Beyond today, beyond my time on earth. For me, God and heaven are the ultimate aspirations.

I believe pain and despair can draw people closer to God. Religious leaders often tell us that suffering with dignity, not rejecting the problems bestowed upon us, is an act that does not go unrewarded. It is sometimes difficult for me to accept this vow, as I know special people who are sick and who will continue to hurt. Some of these souls will die much too early, before the lives they have envisioned are fulfilled. When young people perish after lifetimes fraught with constant pain, it feels wrong, unnatural, and cruel.

* * *

Our daughter, Caitlin, and Jessica (the young woman we met in Lourdes) have become especially close friends. Eighteen months ago, we asked Caitlin if she'd consider meeting up with Jessica for her twenty-third birthday. They were strangers at the time. Jessica lived in LA but was scheduled to visit extended family in Chicago, where Caitlin then lived. Caitlin coordinated a surprise celebration with a group of her work associates and friends. None of the attendees had ever met Jessica, but they showered her with gifts and goodwill. The young woman who'd suffered through so many cancers was overwhelmed by the acts of kindness. Caitlin's bonding with Jessica was instantaneous and has only strengthened.

Caitlin called last week to inform us Jessica was told by doctors that her latest cancer had spread to her lungs and pelvis. The courageous young woman who left an indelible impression upon us from the moment we first met her, who handles her relentless illnesses with such grace, dignity, and faith, had been advised that her time on earth was now more finite.

Here is the list of cancers Jessica has battled since age nine: bone (each leg), breast (double mastectomy), thyroid (removed), and lung. She has withstood countless chemotherapy, radiation, and radiation ablation regimens. Now this news? I lay awake at four o'clock this morning, silently imploring, *But she's just twenty-four years old, for Christ's sake! What about her dreams, her ambitions, her future? You have got to be kidding me! After all her battles, surgeries, and pain? Dammit!*

Caitlin sent me a photo of her and Jessica taken yesterday, their first reunion since the terrible news was delivered, and it was clear to me our daughter had wept prior to the picture being taken. Caitlin was smiling, Jessica was smiling, but there was deep sadness in their eyes. How could there not have been?

Yet, there is also joy amidst Jessica's trials. The joy of knowing we are being touched by a special young spirit who never gives up, who lives each day to the fullest despite enormous uncertainties, who prays for *all* of us, and who is teaching us how *to live*. She reminds us that just because we are ailing doesn't mean we should relinquish hope. Hope for today, hope for our uncertain futures. Jessica exudes not only indomitable courage during her journey here on earth, but unyielding confidence in the promise of eternal life. I don't think the infectious personality realizes the profound effect she is having on so many others.

The recognition that she may be a true saint will inspire me forever; for, what is a saint if not a young person who exemplifies the divine virtues, even during great suffering? *She continues to smile!* I have wondered whether she experiences periods of anger, fear, or misery; after all, she is human. But if she does, I hold her in even greater regard, as her truest essence has remained unwavering.

Thoughts of Jessica's ordeal remind me to again reach out to my sister, Beth. I hope she picks up the phone, but I accept that her pain of losing Sarah is debilitating at times. Beth and her husband, Preston, departed for a night at their lake house but returned home after being informed their precious eighteen-year-old daughter was gone forever. They were committed, loving, and supportive parents to their youngest child. I grieve for them and tremble at the thought of that same horror befalling Karen and me, of having to drive back down the mountain knowing what awaited us.

My mother has lost her parents, her siblings, her husband, and a son, so she understands the depth of Beth's pain. Mom has told me there is no agony surpassing the death of a child. Observing Beth and Preston's crushing sorrow, I know that must be true. Friends and family whose children have died tell me it takes years just to be able to cope with the excruciating permanence of the loss, to fully accept what happened, and to move ahead. But of course, I know, we all know, that each day the aching parent awakens to a sensation that part of them, physically and emotionally, is missing.

Beth is strong, stronger than she realizes. I see her finding her way to reconciliation, to peace. She will endure, just as a mother's love for her lost daughter will endure, forever. But it's an excruciating, meandering process, filled with heartaches.

Tim, a tech industry business associate and friend I was surprisingly reconnected with during the pilgrimage to Lourdes, after years of no communication between us, had once been consumed by a profound anguish few among us will ever have to withstand. In 1981, his best friend—his brother Michael, a twenty-one-year-old with a slight learning disability—was kidnapped by four transients in Colorado Springs. They blindfolded Michael, beat him, and then drove him to a remote mountainside where they stabbed him over sixty times and, because he would not die, they crushed his skull by stomping on his head. It is difficult having to accept that this sort of evil exists in our world.

What is remarkable is that Tim could forgive his brother's assailants, a road that took him years to travel. I pause when asking myself if I could have done what Tim did—bear no more malice toward the brutal killer of a sibling. One of the most difficult aspects of the tragedy for Tim to ponder was that Michael lay tortured with no one present to tell him he was loved, or to hold him as he stopped breathing.

At a dinner with a Jesuit priest on the twenty-five-year anniversary of Michael's death, Tim broke down and told the religious that he still struggled knowing his brother was all alone that fateful day. "Tim, Michael did not die alone," Father Bonfiglio responded. "Jesus was on the hill with him. As Michael cried, Jesus cried; but yet, when Michael took his last breath, Jesus was there and rejoiced to take him home."

No one is ever left alone.

While many of us have our own dilemmas, perhaps we should remind ourselves of the greater suffering of others, so that we can more humbly accept our own circumstances. I respectfully acknowledge that some people with advanced chronic diseases, including MS, may be staring death in the face. My heart goes out to each of them.

Yes, Agnelo[3], sometimes bad things just happen, and our faith can help us to cope.

CHAPTER 25

Sharing Odysseys

We are all flawed, but we all possess wisdom.

ONE OF MY greatest difficulties has been dealing with the loss of coordination and body control that I had taken for granted. There have been mental and emotional assaults, too. Having an illness like mine affects almost everything in one's life. There are so many hurdles to clear each day, it can get exhausting just anticipating—let alone dealing with—those obstacles.

And yet, this became my surprising revelation: I would choose to have lived my life with MS than without it.

I have evolved so much these past thirty years, grown so much because of being stricken, that I wouldn't trade away those lessons. *I am a better human being because of multiple sclerosis.* My priorities for my time here on earth have been reset. I have gotten involved in other peoples' lives, trying to guide them past their own unique troubles. MS has forced me to pay more attention to our world and the people in it. In return, I have been inspired by those walking their own disease journeys.

Life came very easily to me for decades. Of course, I took it all for granted. Moving through airports, malls, or stadiums,

I rarely reflected on the travails of any disadvantaged person I saw along the way. Then I became one of them. Until one gets diagnosed with a chronic disease, it is virtually impossible to appreciate a life encumbered by one.

MS rewards you. It enables you to relate to other struggling people, whether they have been diagnosed with autoimmune illnesses, are facing financial ruin, or dealing with other stresses. I feel obligated to engage such people, to recognize their pain and concerns, and to positively affect lives. I don't mean to infer I am some sort of healer who can offer words and wisdom allowing others to magically overcome their worries, but when someone recognizes that the person listening to them is emotionally invested in understanding their adversities, they tend to value, even to embrace, that person's advice. They connect.

"B. Masters" is a successful high-tech executive. I met him twenty-five years ago, when he was a manager at a company doing business with Intel. It was easy for me to determine that B. Masters was a capable individual, so it was no surprise he was promoted to vice president. Initially, we were solely business acquaintances, but we became friends sharing a passion for college football and fishing. He is an avid SEC fan, and I continue to help him deal with that handicap.

B. would fly out to Oregon every few years for a weekend at our beach house in Pacific City, where we'd share a beer, catch up on each other's family, and try to hook fifty-pound Chinook salmon on the Nestucca River (we hooked but never landed them!).

B. Masters has bipolar disorder, meaning he can experience periods of normal to extreme joy followed by bouts of irritability or depression. I was honored he decided to share his pain, and affected by his account of living with his condition. I was unprepared when he remarked that every morning he awakens, he must convince himself not to take his own life (these thoughts have since abated).

"Wow" was my response. I added that I could not fathom wanting to hurt myself, let alone kill myself. We talked about conquering our fears and dealing with lives touched by MS and mental health disorders. We discussed how our loved ones played critical roles in helping us find and maintain happiness.

We shared the silver linings of our hardships, which always do exist. B. Masters commented that people would sometimes tell him they could "understand how difficult that is" when he disclosed his desperations caused by his bipolar disorder. He said he would occasionally get offended by such commentary, because it highlighted ignorance in grasping the depths of his anguish.

While it's probably true no one can fully relate to contemplations of suicide unless they have held similar thoughts, I reminded him that most people meant well when making such remarks. We can't harshly judge those whose life experiences don't align with our own.

There was common ground between B. Masters and me. We were both active young men who realized we were not fully healthy during our teens or early twenties. We both strove for success because we were competitive and raised to want to achieve goals. After our diagnoses, we were left to ponder the effects our maladies might have on our families, careers, and lifestyles. We were each facing futures of uncertainty, which were sometimes minimally and other times profoundly altered by our ailments.

I reflected on a truth after our discussions. I move awkwardly and rely upon walkers and wheelchairs; I am quickly categorized as not normal, as different. But like B. Masters, there are millions of people whose chronic diseases or mental illnesses are largely invisible to the public. Their anguish must exceed anything I have known. These people often agonize in silence.

"Charles" the Southerner

Charles died much too young. After going on a three-day drinking binge and getting kicked out of resort properties in Orange County, he hired a limo to take him to his residence in Coto de Caza. He instructed the chauffeur to keep the car running while he dashed inside to grab some documents. Charles never made it back to the limo. After rushing upstairs to grab his passport, he tripped and tumbled down the steps, striking his head on the marble foyer below. This is how my good friend Charles the Southerner lost his life.

B. Masters says we all have our crosses to bear. B. Masters's is his bipolar condition. He says mine is multiple sclerosis. Charles the Southerner's cross to bear was his lifelong struggle with alcoholism. But like many among us, Charles's burden was invisible to even his closest friends.

The tragedy of Charles's death was that he had so darn much to live for. He was bright (he liked to remind me his IQ was 142), well-respected, and successful. Charles the Southerner had a slew of great friends he always enjoyed telling me about, and a wonderful wife and family to share his future with.

Charles began drinking while at college in Tennessee. He was a brother of the ΣAE fraternity, and I am sure he was quite the charmer to the young ladies on campus. He was tall, athletic, and distinguished looking when I knew him, so I can only imagine how he must've wowed the coeds. But he drank too much and too often while on campus, he later told me. Thus began his lifelong battle with alcoholism. A battle he lost.

In 1995, Charles invited me on a business trip to Beaver Creek, Colorado. In retrospect, it would be more properly defined as a *boondoggle*. He extended the offer after a meeting attended by me and my Intel boss, Ed. Charles put Ed on the spot by requesting that I attend the "great opportunity to strengthen the bonds between our two companies." Ed replied that he thought it made sense and, as we walked away, he whispered to me, "Make sure you turn this into a worthwhile business activity." (Translation: Don't come home without big orders and strong commitments to Intel products and strategies.) Charles informed us the costs would be minimal, even implying that he or his company would be covering them.

When I arrived at the condo at the base of the slopes, I was amazed by the quality of our lodging and its proximity to the ski lifts, which were literally steps from our door. I commented, "Wow, Charles, you must be spending a fortune on these digs." (Beaver Creek is ridiculously expensive.) He turned to me, smiling, and replied, "Oh it's not bad when you divide it by four people." At that point, I realized my boss Ed was going to flip out when he saw my next expense report. (And he did. The sounds emanating from his office two weeks later were epic entertainment, and included, "@#$%! Tell Cruickshank to get his @$$ in here—now!")

We drank Lagavulin and Schnapps in Colorado. We assumed Charles had, like all us other (paying!) guests, accepted that once we flew home the swigging would stop. We were wrong. It turned out Charles was a heavy drinker who'd been downing Jack Daniel's inside his Porsche on his way to work every morning. He'd been drinking hard liquor during weeknights, alone. I wouldn't have believed it had I not heard it directly from him, divulged just prior to his final alcohol-induced meltdown in Orange County.

During his last revealing visit to Oregon, maybe a decade after we had first met, I picked Charles the Southerner up from Portland International Airport. We proceeded directly to my home so he could meet Karen for the first time. Then Charles and I left for our beach house in Pacific City for what was intended to be a weekend of crabbing, chatting, and dining at the Pelican, Grateful Bread, and Riverhouse restaurants.

Nearing the end of our drive to Pacific City, Charles made a shockingly inappropriate remark about Karen, going well beyond any acceptable commentary on her looks and personality. I pulled over, stunned. "Don't you ever [bleep]ing say anything like that again, Charles. *Ever.*"

It seemed surreal. I wanted to turn around and drop him off at PDX so he could get the hell out of my state, but we were just minutes from our destination. I planned to stop at the Pelican for a bite to eat, where I would again confront him.

I got straight to the point: I wanted an apology and an explanation for what had just happened. I sat there stewing, staring, wanting to punch him in the face, and awaiting his reply. That's when I first glimpsed the depth of Charles's ugly reality.

The retired executive started crying and informed me of lifelong demons related to his alcoholism. He recounted how it had begun in the fraternity, and how it had affected his marriages. He disclosed things he had done in his life that had been influenced by alcohol, and some frightening routines related to his drinking.

He also expressed his sadness about my now-visible MS. But the one thing Charles the Southerner didn't do was apologize. No mention of the inappropriate words he had made about my wife. He wanted to explain his drinking to me; I needed much more than his personal history and sympathy for my health battles. I could not overcome my anger and we ended up having an unpleasant evening followed by his early departure from Oregon.

One or two months later I received an email from Charles

addressed to me and about twenty of his closest friends. As part of his Alcoholics Anonymous rehabilitation and counseling, he had been urged to send a sincere expression of his gratitude for our friendships, and remorse for his behavior toward some of the people copied on the communication. It turns out the fierce exchange I had with Charles wasn't the only disturbing incident among his circle of friends. Charles had been drunk when I picked him up from the airport (I had no idea). He later apologized, effusively, for his words about Karen. I now understood his anguish and the horrors of his addiction. My MS progression seemed trivial in comparison. I knew Charles was fundamentally a good man, and I now realized drinking had sporadically veiled that essence.

Charles retired a millionaire after an impressive career. He owned beautiful homes, cars, and boats. He traveled extensively and treated his third wife and family to wonderful international excursions with lasting memories. The last two years of his life, he talked glowingly to me about his teenage stepchildren and how proud he was of their general goodness. He loved his wife. He wanted to be a rock, a solid foundation for his family into the future.

Instead, he tripped and fell in his own home during a drunken stupor. A tragic ending to any person's life.

*   *   *

While we were in Beaver Creek, I had followed Charles and the other members of our trip up the slopes for a run down the hill. I was not the seasoned skier the other guys were, but I had always enjoyed a sporting challenge. I had not skied for over ten years and my MS had progressed considerably more than I had grasped. I got off the lift and the four of us stared down the steep mountain now freshly laden with light powder. It was beautiful and I was excited.

We took off down the slope and I grew pleased with how my body was adjusting to the sport. But as Charles and I descended, and as I exerted strength and energy to reach our next meeting point, my body temperature rose and my coordination and balance deteriorated. It became obvious it'd be impossible for me to make it to the lodge on a pair of skis.

I told Charles I needed to remove equipment and walk down the mountainside. I was embarrassed. Charles looked at how slowly my body was moving. He lifted his goggles, stared me in the eyes, and graciously offered—insisted, actually—to carry everything back to our (very expensive) condo. I said, "no thanks," but he was unwavering, swinging it all over his shoulders and trekking toward our destination. Charles then spoke to me in an upbeat manner regarding life and our friendship.

This is the Charles I reflect upon.

I have found that a fair percentage of the highly intelligent people I know resist the existence of God. Charles the Southerner, an avowed atheist, would often question my beliefs in Jesus, God, saints, and the afterlife. I always found it interesting that someone so steadfastly opposed to all religion would constantly pick my brain about my faith. We had entirely different views on the topic. We never argued, just amicably agreed to disagree. These discussions have become warm reflections.

I used to rib Charles by threatening to pray for him upon his death, after we both had reached our eighties or nineties. He'd always smirk and reply, "You do that; I love that idea!" After his memorial service, Charles's wife and I agreed that perhaps he just needed to be shown God existed. I smile as I speak-type these words, because I suspect God and Doubting Charles have met, and embraced.

I pray for Charles every evening. He was a generous man. And mischievous. I miss him.

CHAPTER 26

Of Horses, Bookies, and Vegas

Addictions are also progressive diseases.

A T AGE TWENTY-SEVEN, I placed wagers on thirteen NCAA basketball tournament games, figuring at worst I'd split them and owe some *vigorish* (the ten percent cut the bookie takes on every losing bet). But I hoped to win thousands. I didn't watch a single game and lost twelve of thirteen bets. That's supposed to be darn near mathematically impossible to achieve. I didn't have the money readily available to pay George the Bookie, so I called him to discuss the issue, in a panic.

George the Bookie told me he was going to eat the losses but that he never wanted me to wager again. He made me promise, like a parent or spouse might demand. George the Bookie was an outlier; no gambler should ever expect the grace he inexplicably granted me. In the seedy real world of illicit gambling, bookies will get their money. Oh yes, they will. Their toughs will track you down to get the money you owe them. If you do not pay, bad things will happen—just like on TV. This is as true for the employee at Walmart as it is for the professional athlete you see on television.

My good friend "Winston" was sentenced to three years in a federal prison camp for mail fraud. Mail fraud is a broad category of offenses including various felonies, but in short, Winston took millions of dollars that were not his and passed them on to bookies in support of his gambling addiction.

Read this soul-baring narrative from Winston to understand how destructive behavior can evolve:

"In high school I bet $0.25/game with a friend of mine to have "an interest" in each NFL game. About a year out of college, I bet $50/game to have "an interest" in each NFL and college game. By the time my fraudulent activity was uncovered, I was betting $25,000/game to have "an interest" in a game. I wasn't a big casino player, and luckily never opened a line-of-credit with a casino, but I started going to Vegas (with you, Ken) with maybe $200 and playing computer blackjack, to later taking thousands of dollars in cash with me, playing with that cash, while at the same time calling the bookie(s) and placing tens of thousands of dollars of bets, just to get action down."

Do you know somebody who wagers often on sports and who likes to claim, "I'm up overall"? They are almost always lying to you, and to themselves. They are losing money.

As a fresh ASU graduate, I would occasionally fly with Winston from Los Angeles to Las Vegas on a work night, gamble hundreds of dollars, fly back in the morning, and go to work. That's not what I told my parents (I lived at home for a year post-graduation); I'm sure I employed some smokescreen excuse. Gambling was my secret, an ugly habit that worsened.

There are people who instinctively accept that no one can

win money through regular wagering on sports, cards, or dice. People like my wife. She knows the truth. I ultimately accepted the truth. Around the time of my acceptance, I thought Winston had also embraced reality. I was wrong. There are many of us who, for whatever reasons, are unable to admit to the inevitabilities of betting. The degree to which a person cannot accept that all gamblers end up in the red is, in my opinion, what separates the enlightened from those who may become addicted victims. The less they embrace that *the house always wins*, the more dependent and poorer they are likely to become.

While George the Bookie granted me a reprieve, I wasn't so lucky with Karen after my 1987 NCAA basketball tournament nightmare. She told me if I ever bet like that again she would take Kenny (he was our only child at that time) and leave me. *She was serious.* She'll always be a hero to me for her rigid response. Full disclosure: While I never bet big money again, I did relapse on multiple occasions, just to lesser degrees. Thankfully, I one day overcome all betting urges. I am now forced to wonder how Winston's life might have been different had he also been urged by a loved one, or even a bookie, to quit gambling.

Here's more of Winston's reflection:

"I also believe gambling is a way of hiding from yourself and others (which is emotional and has nothing to do with compulsive behavior). I was never an outgoing person, but could always handle myself in public if necessary. The point is, I would rather be by myself, where I could control the environment, as opposed to being around other people, where I couldn't control the environment. Being an introvert, I was never comfortable going to parties in high school and, at times, in college. I felt most comfortable at the track, where I could relax and be myself, by myself. In college, I would take the notes from my class and study for exams while I sat by myself in the grandstand, and while I bet on the races.

To best explain the first 24 or 25 years of my life, I loved to play the dog and horse races in Portland and Phoenix, but never once made a bet with a bookie, until a year or two after I graduated college, and then my life changed. The worst thing to happen to anyone who likes to gamble is to win early on. I believe when I was 24 I placed a $20 bet with a bookie and won $600. When I was 18 I placed a $2 bet on a dog race and won $230, and when I was 19 I bet $30 on a horse race and won just under $5,000. Before I met a bookie the most I could lose was the amount that I had on me. After I met a bookie the most I could lose was whatever amount the two of us decided was my "limit," which to an obsessed gambler is about 10 times more than he can afford to lose. And since bookies made their livings from people like myself, and had no problem accepting payment a few weeks late, they were more than willing to accept my bets."

I wrote a letter to the judge who'd be sentencing Winston to prison. In it, I spoke of a man who is considerate, ethical, moral, and a great father and husband. He is indeed fundamentally all these things. (I understand some people will struggle to accept this.) I have known him since our college days; he is a good man whom I am proud to call my friend. But gambling addiction is a terrible sickness for some.

Winston dwelt on getting his life back under control while serving his sentence. It will be challenging for him to manage the burdens of his cravings, but those who love him will assist in moving beyond the shackles of his dark secret, forever. Winston has a special wife and terrific children he can rebuild his future with. He has everything to live for.

Winston called me from a prison in Southern California during his incarceration. He had been moved temporarily from his facility in Northern California because the government needed some depositions related to his case. I had sent him a long message through the monitored prison email system prior to our phone conversation. In it, I had mentioned what a beautiful day it was outside my home office window. He told me he was profoundly jealous of my opportunity to gaze outside, to appreciate the simple beauty of nature, because his cell had no view and he was in a crowded facility with hardened criminals. It is still difficult to believe he served time.

Road Trips

It was time to visit Winston in prison. The Three Amigos—Dan the Man with his walker, yours truly with his portable scooter, and Good Buddy Ron as designated driver (and whipping boy)—decided to take off on a road trip to Northern California to visit our imprisoned buddy. Winston's facility was in the middle of nowhere, making it difficult for visitors to coordinate stopovers, especially in winter, as the high elevation and road conditions made it precarious to journey there. But it was now summer; it was dry and safe, and we missed our friend. A road trip was clearly necessary.

Ron flew in from Atlanta to pilot my van, with its wheelchair lift, roomy interior, and great selection of freshly burned CDs, on a thousand-mile journey to a prison located between Susanville, California, and Reno, Nevada. Three middle-aged men reunited for a few days of driving and storytelling as we traveled to visit a man paying back his debt to society. The last time the four of us were together, we were on a cruise ship in the Western Caribbean, drinking mojitos and eating hamburgers on deck.

Ron, Dan, and I talked for ten and a half hours as we trekked south on I-5. We retold stories from the past thirty years. Some of the retellings were slightly embellished, and all of them brought smiles to our faces. The only thing interrupting our exaggerations was the need for a real lunch, as eating mixed nuts, dried fruit, and Cheetos had lost its luster. We stopped in Klamath Falls, Oregon, which is also in the middle of nowhere, and ordered the one meal rational people would ordinarily steer clear of in a small mountain town located far from sea on a hot day: tuna fish sandwiches. The truth is, we were so famished, those darn Chicken of the Sea preparations tasted out of this world. With our bellies filled, it was time to continue our travels.

The second statement Winston made upon our arrival to the work camp facility was, "Prison sucks the life out of a person." Of course, it was difficult for us to see him incarcerated in his orange jumpsuit. Still, we felt good about making him smile as we once again shared absurd college and road trip stories, beginning the process of turning our trip to visit him into a classic memory.

Winston told us that the other prisoners had been amused by the sight of us meandering toward the facility's entrance; he said it reminded him of a *Seinfeld* episode. Three Goofy Amigos making their way through a desert parking lot to a federal prison: the healthy guy; the walker guy; the scooter guy. Winston stated that the prisoners looking through the compound's windows were wondering who the comical trio was coming to visit; he was forced to come clean and claim association with the gimpy posse.

One year later, we made our second trip to visit Winston. My MS had progressed a bit further, Dan the Man's condition had similarly worsened, and Good Buddy Ron broke an even bigger sweat loading us into and out of cars and hotel rooms. We understood Winston needed company, and we also accepted we had a responsibility to do what we could to ease his time in prison. No one said as much in the car, but I'm sure each of us held the same thought: This was the least we could do. Not only for Winston, but for his family. We were later told our visits helped lighten the burden of guilt and loneliness he had experienced.

*   *   *

Something struck me as I was shaving the other day. Winston and I have this in common: We will be living the rest of our lives with chronic afflictions, my multiple sclerosis and his deeply embedded gambling disorder. Some people might deride this comparison, but the more I contemplated our circumstances, the stronger the similarities became.

MS is often perceived to be predominately a physical challenge, but anyone with the disease will tell you many of its most difficult facets are mental. Do I have to change my career? Have I left my family in a sound financial situation? Will I be able to stay positive and productive as I move through the various stages of MS? Aren't these some of the same questions Winston could be asking?

I didn't choose to have MS. Winston never raised his hand to volunteer to become a deeply addicted gambler. Yes, he chose to wager, but not to evolve into an obsessed casualty. I hope we will both have the determination necessary to build or maintain bright futures for our families and ourselves. I believe we will.

Winston is now a free man. He holds a BA and certifications representing his skills in finance and accounting. He has secured employment, his first step toward rebuilding his career. He and his family are successfully transitioning to a content life. Winston deserves his second chance at a normal, productive, and gratifying future.

Aren't we all seeking some sort of redemption?

CHAPTER 27

ALS Steals a Good Man

It was hard to watch.

A T AGES THIRTY-NINE and forty, I spent two separate weeks-long stints at what is today called the Sierra Integrative Medical Center (SIMC), in Reno. While there, I met people who were suffering from seemingly every disease known to exist. The care at the facility was expensive and, because it was not a Western medicine clinic utilizing exclusively Western-approved drugs and protocols, most of the bills for the patients I met there were paid for out of pocket; insurance companies typically declined the claims. Some of these people would have handed over every dollar they had: They were desperate. Desperate for cures, desperate for prolonged lives.

The lead doctor at SIMC during my treatments was a fascinating woman named Dr. Lee. She held medical degrees from impressive institutions in Taiwan and the United States. Accordingly, she and her staff employed a unique approach to treating the diseased walking through their doors, typically integrating Western and Eastern protocols. For some, the results were extraordinary.

I met an Eastern Orthodox priest who believed he had been cured of his cancer at SIMC. Many MSers swore their symptoms had lessened, even disappeared. Lyme disease and chronic fatigue patients insisted they, too, had been healed. For others, the desperation leading them to Reno from around the world was, sadly, not answered by significant improvements or elimination of their ailments.

My personal experiences at SIMC were thus: I did appear to have been slightly improved during both of my weeks-long treatments at the clinic, which might be extraordinary, as there were no drugs available at that time that specifically targeted PPMS.

At one point, having a mercury-filled tooth extracted (Dr. Lee believed it was interfering with my healing), I thought I had been miraculously cured. Excruciatingly, the very real improvements I had instantaneously felt throughout the left side of my body after the tooth extraction lasted only a few minutes. I will never forget those remarkable ticks of the clock. When the sensations of my MS returned, as my body regained its struggling state, the world seemed crueler to me.

My MS doctor-researcher at Oregon Health Sciences University (OHSU) believed it was possible I had slightly improved after my care at SIMC, but he made a valid comment: The doctors and staff at the center in Reno had employed such a vast array of medicines and treatments (such as hyperbaric oxygen chambers, hours-long infusions of natural remedies, myriad custom homeopathic medicines), it would have been nearly impossible to determine which treatment had delivered which correlating benefit.

Part of me wished I could have received their treatments every day for years, but they were so expensive it was an unreasonable consideration. A person would have to spend millions of dollars for a lifetime of such care.

*   *   *

I met Jeff the Farmer and his wife, Christie, at SIMC in 2000 or 2001. They were Missourians. Jeff had been diagnosed with ALS a year earlier and he was desperate to find a cure that would assuage contemplations of leaving Christie and their three young children alone. He was a tall man, I am guessing about six-three, and by the time I met him he was noticeably underweight. Jeff was a farmer by trade and, after sharing stories from our youths, we agreed we would've had great times hanging out together twenty years earlier—we would have gotten into all sorts of trouble.

Jeff the Farmer was a storyteller. One of his most entertaining accounts involved his ex-wife (or ex-girlfriend; I'm hazy on that detail). He had received a frantic phone call from her one evening; she was screaming about a man who was "going crazy" on her front porch, threatening to break the door down. Jeff hopped into his truck and tore down the road toward the damsel in distress's house.

When he arrived, she and the unwelcome suitor were in the midst of a raging argument. After unsuccessfully attempting to negotiate with the volatile ex, Jeff went into the woman's bedroom and grabbed a shotgun, assuming he could mandate peace and order with the sight of a Winchester twelve-gauge.

Unfortunately, even after Jeff had informed the man that he would be shot if he continued attempting to take the woman from the property, the aggressor foolishly threw caution to the wind, lifted her over his shoulder, and carried her down the steps toward his car. Jeff yelled out one final warning.

The pleas were disregarded so Jeff shot him, right in the ass. *Bang!* At this point in the storytelling I exclaimed, "Come on, Jeff, you're yanking my chain. This isn't true!" He calmly replied, "Yep, it's all true, Ken." I told him I was surprised he hadn't been arrested for attempted murder, to which he responded he lived in a small town with small town (he called it *uncorrupted*) justice. Because he was only trying to protect the woman, the legal system powers that be decided any charges were unwarranted. He spent only hours in jail.

Jeff told me the victim, now sporting a scar in one of his butt cheeks, had attended a wedding that Jeff had also been present at, a couple of years after the shooting incident. Jeff said he exerted great effort to enjoy the festivities, but that every time he'd glance at the angry shotgun victim, the man would glare back intimidatingly. "I really thought he might shoot me in retribution."

I am sometimes advised that my sense of humor is appreciated by me alone, but I honestly consider Jeff's story a classic. Thanks for sharing it, my friend.

Jeff introduced me to the recreational sport of *noodling* for catfish. I'd never heard of such a thing but quickly grew captivated by its description: In the summer months along the shores of Missouri lakes and rivers that catfish nest in, a *noodler* sticks his hands down into holes the fish have burrowed into, and when the catfish bites his probing fingers, the struggle begins. He described how some of the guys he'd gone noodling with had received deep wounds and bloodied appendages trying to yank fifty-pound catfish from their watery nests. It sounded like just my kind of fun; perhaps I needed to take a trip to Missouri.

Jeff the Farmer, Christie, and I developed a bond during our time together at the clinic. It was difficult watching him struggle, hopeful that doctors could cure his ALS. But ultimately, he traveled back to his farm in Missouri to spend his final days with his family.

During that time, Jeff had contemplated his end. One day he'd decided that just waiting for his disease to kill him was not the way he wanted to leave this world. So Jeff the Farmer, his body now withered, swallowed his entire supply of morphine, walked down the hall toward Christie, tossed her the empty container, and prepared himself for one final consoling at her side. He had made sure their young children would not be home during his passage to the afterlife.

Christie stayed true to her husband's wishes, trying to comfort him until his last breath had been taken. It was not an easy passing. Many elderly or ailing persons will die quietly, peacefully. But some of our bodies will struggle for survival, perhaps even after our souls have already departed.

I sometimes reflect on how Jeff's closing hours must have been traumatizing to Christie. Such accounts remind me to ensure, to the extent I can, that my passing will be as comfortable as doctors and hospice caregivers can possibly make it for me *and* my family.

I cannot imagine making the decision Jeff did. I think it's imperative to try to stay positive while dealing with any disease, especially during the most difficult moments. But I make no moral judgments regarding Jeff's final act. How could I?

Jeff the Farmer was a good man who loved his family and loved God. He was a prolific poet who left me one of his works, verses of a lonely cowboy at Christmastime. His trademark message to me and others was "Because nice matters," which he repeated often. He was mild and kind, and desperately sought a cure to continue his life here on earth with his wife and kids. That was not to be.

I think about Jeff and Christie often.

CHAPTER 28

Why Are the Women Crying?

"The greatest evil is physical pain."
—St. Augustine

MY INITIAL VISIT to the alternative medical clinic in Reno perplexed me. As I sat in the facility's waiting room, I noticed several women with tears in their eyes, at nine in the morning. Had they each just received some terrible news? Were they frightened by medical procedures scheduled for later in the day? I tried to be inconspicuous, occasionally glancing at their anguished faces through the tinted lenses of my Ray-Bans.

I eventually realized these same women were sometimes in tears not just in the mornings, but later in the afternoons. I was being exposed to one of the most challenging aspects of dealing with a life touched by multiple sclerosis and many other autoimmune diseases: pain.

Most people afflicted with MS experience periods of clinically significant or chronic pain. Researchers have learned there is total randomness regarding which MSers will be encumbered by any real agony. How old a person is, when she was diagnosed, and her level of disability are not factors corresponding to her levels of pain.

Some of these women at the clinic suffered from stinging sensations stretching down their spines, others from feelings of electric shocks assailing their faces. They told me spasms, and what felt like burning skin or joints, were at times debilitating. When I got to know several of these ladies better, I found myself awestruck by their perseverance and outlooks in the face of such suffering.

The only other time I've seen a woman's face mutely express such penetrating physical pain was when Karen struggled with her own severe discomfort. She had torn tendons and nerves near the base of her spine and had become completely incapacitated; even minimal efforts to move delivered unbearable hurt. At one point during her episode, I walked into our master bedroom and found her sitting on a wingback chair, still as night, tears streaming down her face. She couldn't speak.

Sometimes the aching is almost fully hidden. I once worked with an MSer named Valerie, and I recall her telling me she experienced Level 8 pain during portions of every day, either at work or home. Many people have had The Pain Chart explained to them by a nurse or doctor before or after medical treatments. For those who have not, here's some perspective on what Val was coping with:

Level 8: Intense pain. Physical activity is severely limited. Conversing requires great effort.

Val was a warrior who somehow persevered. If she wept, she did so out of her coworkers' sight. I don't know if the distress the women at the clinic were dealing with was greater than Val's chronic or Karen's temporary suffering; I only know it was overwhelming, that it forced them to endure their trials in silence, with tears cascading over their cheeks. Day after day.

While many of those with MS, Parkinson's, or ALS are dealing with unrelenting pain, I'm one of the fortunate, because the burning, pin pricks, spasms, back pains, and more are only uncomfortable for me. For half of those afflicted with multiple sclerosis, those same symptoms can be oppressive. It's all about how our brains interpret the nerve signals flowing in from the affected areas.

I do not believe women are less capable of handling the pain of MS than men are. While I have encountered many more women than men afflicted with autoimmune diseases, I have seen few differences between the sexes when it comes to dealing with physical discomfort.

Why were they crying in the clinic? Because they were hurting. If someone with chronic disease tells you they are in agony—believe them.

* * *

A Queen

For some, just getting through the day is a worthy accomplishment.

I observed an impressive woman while receiving therapy after my hip replacement surgery in 2010. I grew awed by her grace and strength displayed under her difficult circumstances. Appearing to be about forty, she was strong-willed, attractive, and unusually fit for a woman in her challenged state. The best word I can use to describe her is *noble.*

One of the therapists helping me recover after my surgery explained that the stranger in question was also battling primary progressive MS. Like me, she was bound to a wheelchair and used a walker sparingly. She was healing from an operation, perhaps the same procedure I had just undergone.

What moved me most was the way she held her head high, expressing herself with class and dignity, despite her many obvious adversities. She exerted great effort to become more independent through her therapy. She exuded strength of character, even during what would be termed moments of embarrassment by many of us: having to deal with adult diapers that were impossible for her to fully conceal.

She did improve during our time together, tiny advances in strength, balance, and coordination. I caught her glancing at me while I was trying to perform the same exercises that were part of her daily rehab routine. Two strangers sharing the journey. I watched her force herself to stand, walk, and exercise as best she could, which wasn't very well. I never saw her suggest any want for sympathy. This woman never lost her self-esteem, her sense of self-worth, her nobility. She was formidable. A queen.

We were both so deeply immersed in our bids to regain basic independence that we inevitably reached the point where one of us had made enough progress to warrant release. One afternoon, I was wheeled out of the hospital for a reunion with my family, never to see her again.

Karen and our kids visited me often in the hospital, but I didn't notice a single person at the queen's side during my stay there. Not in the halls, in rehabilitation rooms, or at meal times. No spouse, partner, or friend. No emotional or physical support from the people she knew. *She was alone!* No one's supposed to travel this road unaccompanied.

I often check to see if the women with MS I run into at various clinics or hospitals are wearing any wedding rings; I am not looking for a second wife. I had long-ago concluded that many ladies with multiple sclerosis ultimately end up companionless. The data confirms it: A much greater percentage of women with MS get divorced or otherwise abandoned versus afflicted men. It's a sad truth.

PART V
Hope

*"Hope is a good thing, maybe the best of things,
and no good thing ever dies."*
—*The Shawshank Redemption*

CHAPTER 29

Interconnectedness

"You, my darling, have shown me God,
and you have shown me heaven."
—Dr. M

TWO OF THE *malades* (the ill) who left a strong impression on me during our pilgrimage to Lourdes died after our return to Oregon. Steve, a father from Seattle battling advanced cancer, succumbed soon after our return. I'll never forget him drawing a picture on a napkin after a meal in France. We had just finished a conversation about both of our families' children, and about the optimism and dreams we have for their futures. He wrote a single word inside each of three circles, pushed the paper across the table, and then he emphasized the foundations he believed were essential to providing young people fulfilling lives: faith in themselves, faith in their partner, and faith in God.

Karen and I also grieved the loss of a ten-year-old boy, Dominic, months after our return. He wore a patch over one eye in France because sensitivity to light exacerbated the pain caused by his brain tumor. We spent time with him and his parents during breakfast one morning, and though Dominic said little, he deeply affected me. I sensed great kindness in the child. That night, at two in the morning, Dominic woke his father and asked to be taken to the shrine of Our Lady.

Imagine walking your extremely ill child in the middle of the night toward a religious site you consider particularly holy. Contemplate holding him tightly, asking for a miracle, or the strength to deal with a worst-case scenario: his death. Envision shedding tears of love and of weariness for whatever lay ahead. I hope Dominic's parents will find some comfort reflecting on a father's precious time with his sick son at the base of the statue of Mary.

One afternoon in Lourdes, all the *malades* of the Western Association of the US Order of Malta gathered together for the opportunity to present our health journeys, and to listen to others confronting similar difficulties. I witnessed anger, fear, and confusion as some of the struggling *malades* began to share their stories. Their accounts tore my heart out. My problems seemed minuscule compared to what many of these folks were dealing with.

After several tragic and heart-wrenching stories had been presented, and as many people in the room were shedding tears (for themselves, perhaps, but I suspect mostly for others), a woman named Regina stood up to tell her story. Even before she began speaking, I noted the compassion emanating from her face and eyes.

Regina informed us that, twenty years earlier, she had been pregnant with twins who had developed ectopically (outside the uterus). One day she suddenly began hemorrhaging and was rushed to the hospital, where she bled out on a table in an emergency room. She lost the twins and her heart monitor flatlined. Doctors and nurses attempted to resuscitate her, even pounding on her chest. No heartbeat, no breathing, no vitals.

As medics continued scrambling, Regina's soul floated

up: She was watching her own drama unfold. She was then enveloped by a love she told us was beyond our comprehension. A love so strong, she believed (I will never forget her words) "*it would crush a human body.*" That love, she told us, was God. She did not want to return to our world, but, while hoping to be embraced by God for eternity, her mind told her to *watch the nurse's fist.* As she did so, the fist crashed onto her lifeless body's chest, and she descended from above. Her heartbeat returned. She was alive.

I am too often a skeptic. Maybe it is because, as one of ten children, I had been subjected to all sorts of exaggerated tales delivered by nine siblings (I subjected them to my own). But I grew up and became, I believe, adept at judging people's accounts of moments they'd witnessed or been part of. Regina's story was delivered with unflappable confidence and penetrating resoluteness. She was unwavering. And besides, I asked myself, why would a person make this up?

This was Regina's second pilgrimage to Lourdes; she was now battling Stage III cancer. Though not a member of my team, I found myself in her presence often; in churches, at meals, and on tours. The word I'd use to describe her is *holy*. Her final message to the room full of *malades* on the day she first told her story was: *Do not be afraid to die.* She said we are destined for something more wonderful than we could ever imagine.

On our last evening in France, after the life-changing week, Regina retold her incredible account to the entire US contingent of the Order of Malta. Her narrative was again delivered unflinchingly, every detail presented exactly as it had been the first time.

Three weeks later, I received an email informing me Regina's cancer had disappeared soon after arriving home from Lourdes, baffling her doctors. Again, truth is stranger than fiction.

After my sister Beth and her husband lost their daughter Sarah in 2014, two years after our pilgrimage to Lourdes, we flew south for the funeral, which was held in Beth and Preston's backyard in Orange County, and attended by over six hundred family members and friends. Karen and I were very surprised to find Dr. M at the service, a woman we'd met in Lourdes, and whose husband was struggling with ALS.

We learned that Dr. M had been one of Sarah's medical specialists during the previous year. The doctor conveyed shock that Sarah, a vibrant young woman with so much promise, whose life had settled into a wonderful phase, had been pulled from our world through tragic circumstances.

After the funeral, I reflected upon the last evening in Lourdes with Dr. M and the Order of Malta, during which Dr. M was the closing speaker. She rose from her table and spoke about doubts she had harbored, hesitancies related to God that her science education and secular society had pushed her to struggle with. She commented about how her husband's unyielding faith, sustained during his battle against an insidious disease, was transformative for her.

She turned to him, paused, and then said, *"You, my darling, have shown me God, and you have shown me heaven."*

In 2015, I was saddened by an email I received, informing me that Dr. M's husband had lost his battle with ALS.

CHAPTER 30

Enlightenment

Love, compassion, forgiveness, and charity.
Nothing else really matters.

M Y LIFE MOVES forward with disease, uncertainty, and hope. Hope that I am setting a worthy example for those I love. Hope that those struggling more than me will find comfort and optimism for their own futures. Hope that we will all one day be cured of whatever ails us.

Challenges remain. I feel as if the tightrope I am perched on has been raised one hundred feet, and that buffeting winds are picking up. I'm doing everything I can, physically and emotionally, to stay balanced on a swaying line. I'm trying not to fall.

I am not frightened. I am concerned.

Occasionally, I get frustrated by my inability to perform basic tasks. My legs and arms are slowly becoming less functional. Two days ago, I was so exasperated with not being able to plug my headset into my computer that, after five minutes of failed effort, I released a colorful, damning outburst. I had assumed I was home alone—a flawed notion. Karen heard my lashing words.

Later, I sensed she was bothered by the incident, perhaps wondering if my self-mockery was a truer reflection of my daily state of mind. It was not. It was just a fleeting moment exposing my frustration with how disease has permeated my life. Sometimes I need such verbal liberations.

I intend to stay positive as my condition worsens; my demeanor is something I control. But I have great compassion for those who struggle to find light as they walk their difficult roads paved with chronic illness or other misfortune. If asked for insight based on my own experiences, I would tell others the same thing I tell myself: Never give up. There is always meaning and goodness somewhere in our lives. Always. Persevering with hope is a worthy pursuit that sets an upbeat tone that can sustain us long-term.

In early 2016, we attended the funeral of Jessica Bailey, the beautiful young woman I introduced earlier. Her sixth cancer had proved too much; a ravaged body simply gave out at age twenty-five. Our family visited Jessica in Southern California three weeks before she passed. Caitlin flew back and forth from New York to Los Angeles three times in a month to console and, ultimately, say goodbye to a best friend.

Jessica never gave up, never felt sorry for herself. All who knew her were in awe of her unyielding hope and love for others. She held a deep devotion to Jesus and Our Lady of Lourdes. I wish every person reading these pages could have met her, talked to her, been touched by her. Perhaps you have crossed paths with a Jessica sometime during your life. Such people are gifts to humanity.

Jessica's final days in the hospital extended far beyond what doctors and nurses had expected. The medical staff called her protracted transition "beyond human abilities." It was difficult to so intimately view her preparations for death, but she left us all one final, remarkable inspiration. Hours before she took her last breath, her emaciated body lying limp on a hospital bed, she became sporadically animated for seconds at a time. These are the words she repeated to some of her family: "It's so beautiful," and "Wow, it's the best." Jessica's glimpse into everything many of us hope for: heaven.

I've learned that most people are good and beautiful. I'm noticeably impaired, obviously unhealthy, so perhaps my condition has triggered some of the kindness strangers have offered me. But that's probably selling societies short. We are bombarded by images and commentary of mankind's deficiencies, which I feel obscures the quiet decency of billions. Through illness, I've been privileged to have witnessed the truer essence of man.

I think I now have a solid bead on what's most important, illuminated by personal experiences and the wisdom of young and old alike. I owe it to those who have brightened my days through their words and actions to offer courage and compassion to others for the rest of my days (which I hope will exceed ten thousand more!).

Karen recently asked me if I remembered what I had told her soon after being diagnosed with multiple sclerosis, nearly twenty-five years ago. I couldn't recall the conversation, but I considered what I *hoped* I would have said, and I blurted out my response. At the same time, she uttered the words I had spoken that day: *"MS can't take my family and my faith."* Our replies were nearly identical.

When I began this memoir, I had no intention of discussing any religious convictions. While editing the evolving manuscript, I grew surprised by how often I had mentioned my faith as a guiding light. This isn't the only way to deal with a life of disease. It is my way.

I've discovered that through suffering we are exposed to greater love—for and from others. Physical and emotional anguish have enhanced my empathy and sympathy for the ailing, prompted gratitude for my good fortune, and helped me find deeper meaning in my life. Vulnerability has been a gift.

There are times when I've told God I've been sufficiently enlightened by the benefits of my miseries (I accept that my problems pale in comparison to those of so many others), and that the point needs no further emphasis. In other words, could He please heal me now? I believe He's responded.

Do I wish I did not have MS today? Yes, I wish it would disappear. Do I wish I never had MS? No, I do not. I am a better person, in ways that matter most, because of my disease. I would never trade what I've learned and how I've evolved for a lifetime of perfect health. Just as I appreciate how the pursuit of writing has given my present days more dimension, my journey of sickness has led to a life with greater significance.

I have presented instances where I've agonized and reacted poorly to circumstances and events—my moments of weakness. You've read about the greater travails of people I've encountered during my odyssey: Sarah, Jessica, Danny, Chris, and others. Journeys punctuated by heartbreak, but defined by enduring love.

I pray for the sick. I grieve for the parents of those battling incurable illnesses, or whose children have died. It seems so wrong, so unfair, and so senseless for kids and young adults to be stricken by life-threatening illnesses. I trust that one day we will understand the truths of why such painful mysteries exist.

This memoir was not a self-help guide. I never intended it to be a recipe for better living, for the ailing or the healthy. Each chapter was just a snapshot of my life as an MS man, or the lives of those walking parallel paths. I have been the beneficiary of circumstances that forced me to slow down, to gain important insights, and to grow as a person.

I may be the luckiest man in the world. I sincerely mean that. I hold fond memories of growing up in Tustin with nine siblings and two fascinating parents. I smile when recalling my obstreperous youth. My college buddies and I still grin as we reminisce about wild shenanigans—most of which actually happened. I enjoyed my teammates and can still remember that play, that game, or that tournament. I relished my tech career and met wonderful people through it. We've lived in beautiful cities and have traveled to interesting places.

True, I can no longer stand, hold a glass with one hand, or get dressed by myself. It is natural to take such things for granted, until they become impossible. However, my family and I have learned to not only cope with my failing body, but to thrive as a team that is always looking forward.

Our children make me proud beyond words. It was difficult for them to watch their father struggle with his transformation from a healthy body to one that is weak and failing, particularly during their adolescence. Perhaps it is still difficult. But they persevered and are now stronger and more compassionate because of those experiences.

I'm constantly telling people how fortunate I was to have found Karen. She is my hero of my story. Her kindness and courage are pillars of strength for our family. She is my caregiver and my light. I think as much as anything else, the story you've just read might be our love story.

There are thirty million other Americans suffering from serious chronic diseases. The baby boomer generation is aging; many of them will become infirm, requiring the daily physical and emotional support of friends and family. I hope I've done a worthy job of not only presenting the trials and realities of living with disease, but of the rewards of being inspired and fulfilled by a loving caregiver.

I keep dreaming. We keep dreaming. The kids are gainfully employed with jobs they love. Karen's art will be exhibited at Basic Space Gallery tomorrow night, and the State Department has selected her paintings for display at the US Embassy in Bucharest, Romania. I'm still fine-tuning my psychological thriller, and I've just completed this memoir. Art and writing: two boundless passions we can pursue the rest of our days. We're looking for a small place in Arizona to spend the winters. We have weddings and grandchildren (many, I hope) to look forward to.

I've just read an update about Ocrevus™, a new drug that received FDA approval as a treatment for primary progressive multiple sclerosis. It would be the first medication in the world to treat those with PPMS, like me. The trial results are being described with exciting words: "dramatic," "promising," and "breakthrough." I'll be getting infused with Ocrevus[4] in 2018. There *is* always hope.

But whether or not medicine changes my life, I'm smiling. Why shouldn't I be? I've decided the future's going to be stellar.

Take that, MS.

Endnotes

1. The Order of Malta is a fascinating Catholic organization dating back to the time of Christ. Its members are an impressive coalition of successful men and women volunteering inordinate time to their religious work, which includes accompanying ailing Catholics on an annual pilgrimage to the grotto of Our Lady of Lourdes, in France.

2. Grace's parents, Kristin and Matt Wilsey, launched the Grace Science Foundation, whose charter is not only to seek treatments and a cure for the rare NGLY 1 genetic deficiency their daughter inherited, but to seek solutions for myriad diseases. The organization's tagline is "Rare is not an excuse." To read more about the charity's goals and research, check out its website: www.gracescience.org

3. Agnelo Gomes is a friend and priest of The Order of St. Francis Xavier, a good man who builds bridges among people of various faiths and cultures. He is extraordinarily talented; an artist, musician, and documentary film director/producer. One of his gifts is changing lives through dialogue, compassion and wisdom.

4. Genentech is the manufacturer of the potentially breakthrough relapsing remitting and primary progressive multiple sclerosis drug Ocrevus™.

Thank you for reading my memoir!
Perhaps you've found something relevant and worthy
within its pages.

Reviews left on Goodreads or Amazon are greatly appreciated.

I write and edit every day, creating fiction and nonfiction
manuscripts, so stay tuned . . .
Cheers from Oregon,
Ken Cruickshank

www.KenCruickshank.com
www.facebook.com/KenCruickshankAuthor

44435635R00141

Made in the USA
San Bernardino, CA
19 July 2019